"I love Matthew Harmon's book probably because Matt loves the beautiful balance between Bible st he links all his insights to the gospel."

Randy Newman, senior teaching fellow, C. S. Lewis Institute; author, *Questioning Evangelism* and *Corner Conversations*

"I love this book on how to study and apply the Bible. Some books on interpreting Scripture are so complicated and have so many steps that we can become discouraged, but Harmon is simple and clear without being simplistic. He helps us see the big picture in studying the Bible by reminding us of the storyline of Scripture and by emphasizing that the story centers on Jesus himself. At the same time, we are given very practical advice on how to study and apply specific passages. An excellent resource for teachers, students, and all who desire to study the Scriptures."

Thomas R. Schreiner, professor of New Testament, The Southern Baptist Theological Seminary

"The guidance Harmon provides in *Asking the Right Questions* is simple enough for a teenager or new believer to follow, but deep enough to lead even mature Christians to a better grasp and deeper application of Scripture. I love this book and look forward to using it to disciple people in our church."

Brian G. Hedges, lead pastor, Fulkerson Park Baptist Church, Niles, Michigan; author, *Christ Formed in You*

"Asking good questions is a key to understanding. And asking good questions about the Bible is a key to understanding the most important truths in the world. God can handle all your questions, and he loves to reward those who ask in faith when engaging his very words. This book will help you ask the best of questions on the best of sources—God's Word—in the best of ways—by faith."

David Mathis, executive editor, desiringGod.org; pastor, Cities Church, Minneapolis, Minnesota; author, *Habits of Grace: Enjoying Jesus through the Spiritual Disciplines*

Asking the Right Questions

ASKING THE RIGHT QUESTIONS

A Practical Guide to Understanding
and Applying the Bible

MATTHEW S. HARMON

CROSSWAY

WHEATON, ILLINOIS

Library of Congress Cataloging-in-Publication Data

Names: Harmon, Matthew S., author.
Title: Asking the right questions: a practical guide to understanding and applying the Bible / Matthew S. Harmon.
Description: Wheaton: Crossway, 2017. | Includes bibliographical references and index.
Identifiers: LCCN 2016045619 (print) | LCCN 2017013276 (ebook) | ISBN 9781433554308 (pdf) | ISBN 9781433554315 (mobi) | ISBN 9781433554322 (epub) | ISBN 9781433554292 (tp)
Subjects: LCSH: Bible—Criticism, interpretation, etc.
Classification: LCC BS511.3 (ebook) | LCC BS511.3 .H375 2017 (print) | DDC 220.601—dc23
LC record available at https://lccn.loc.gov/2016045619

To the King of the ages,
immortal, invisible, the only God,
be honor and glory forever and ever. Amen.

Contents

ADDITIONAL RESOURCES

Acknowledgments

The Bible is the most remarkable book in the world. The moment God saved me, he gave me a love for his Word. From that point forward, he also brought a number of people into my life who helped me understand and apply the Bible. In high school and college, I had men like Don Willeman, Mike Thacker, and Brian McCollister who discipled me with open Bible in hand. They showed me the beauty of Christ and what it meant to follow him by constantly taking me to Scripture and living out the truths of the Bible right before my eyes.

I also owe a debt of gratitude to several professors who have shaped the way I read the Bible. While studying at Trinity Evangelical Divinity School and Wheaton College, I had the privilege of studying under scholars such as D. A. Carson, Doug Moo, and Greg Beale. Each of them has shaped my study of the Bible in significant ways.

While I was doing my graduate work, I also had multiple opportunities to teach Cru staff how to interpret and communicate the Bible in their various ministries. I taught alongside godly men such as Keith Johnson, Gary Purdy, Rick Hove, Jonathan Pennington, Darian Lockett, and many others. Readers who have gone through those Cru classes will see its fingerprints throughout this book.

As a professor at Grace College and Theological Seminary, I have the privilege of teaching students how to understand and apply the Bible. Much of the material in this book has been used and refined through my interaction with them. The same is true of the many opportunities I have had to teach and preach at Christ's Covenant Church. Seeing God's people grow in their understanding of God's Word and watching them apply it to their lives brings me unspeakable joy.

I also want to express my gratitude to several people who read all or part of this book and gave helpful feedback. Special thanks go to Zac Hess, John Sloat, Gabe Tribbett, and Brian Hedges. Through their thoughtful input they have made this a better book.

Working with the people at Crossway has been a delight. I appreciate their enthusiasm for this project and their help along the way. I owe special thanks to Justin Taylor for his friendship and his encouragement.

Without the love and support of my wife, Kate, and my sons, Jon and Jake, this book would never have been written. They have consistently embraced God's call on my life to help people see the beauty of Jesus Christ and follow him. It is my prayer that God will use this book to make that happen in your life.

Introduction

Her excitement was contagious. Mallika had been a Christian for only a few months, but already her life was beginning to change. She had a newfound joy and peace that transcended her circumstances. If the doors of her local church were open, she was likely there. She loved to sing the hymns and worship songs she was learning. Throughout the day she found herself spontaneously praying about situations and people. She was even beginning to talk to her coworkers and neighbors about Jesus. Since she had grown up in a non-Christian home, everything about her relationship with Jesus Christ was new.

There was just one problem—she had no idea how to understand the Bible and apply it to her life. The woman who led her to Christ emphasized the importance of being in the Word on a regular basis, but had not given Mallika any help or training in how to do this. Every Sunday her pastor faithfully preached the Bible and encouraged the congregation to study Scripture on their own, but just the thought of it completely overwhelmed Mallika. Every time she tried to read her Bible, she just became more discouraged.

Laura has been a believer since she was eight years old. Her parents regularly read the Bible with her and encouraged her involvement in the church's youth ministry. When it came time to choose a college, Laura opted for a small Christian liberal arts college where she knew she would have lots of opportunities to grow in her faith. From her first day on campus Laura was involved in several different ministries at school and her local church.

Despite her constant involvement in ministry, however, Laura struggled to maintain consistent time in God's Word on her own. She enjoyed hearing the messages in chapel and the sermons from the pastor at her church. At times she even attended a Sunday school class. But when she sat down to read and apply the Bible herself, she regularly walked away frustrated. Laura even took an elective class on how to study the Bible, but the method her professor taught was so complicated that she never had the time for it.

After several years of being a member at his church, Tobe was asked to lead a small group. He had come to faith in Christ in his early thirties and has been involved in the church for the past fifteen years. While he is no Bible scholar, Tobe spends time reading the Bible nearly every day. On occasion he even reads Christian books that deepen his understanding of the Bible and how to live the Christian life.

Each week when his small group meets to talk about that week's sermon and the passage on which it is based, however, Tobe often walks away disappointed or even frustrated. Too often their discussions wander down rabbit trails that have little or nothing to do with what the passage says. Or the conversation stays on the surface level and never gets around to how the truths of that passage should change our lives.

• • •

Maybe you can identify with Mallika, Laura, or Tobe because you have had a similar experience. But even if your experience is different, all of us at some point have struggled to know how to understand and apply the Bible to our everyday lives. We believe that understanding and applying the Bible is crucial to following Jesus, but we don't always feel equipped to do it well.

Why is something so important to the Christian life so hard sometimes? For one thing, the Bible is a big book that talks about a lot of different things. How do you figure out the most important things to look for when reading it?

To read any book well you need to know what kind of book it is. So what kind of book is the Bible? Why did God give it to us? Does the Bible give us any help in knowing how to read it?

Another reason understanding and applying the Bible can be challenging is that the Bible is set in a world very different from today. Some of the stories and people it describes seem very strange or even upsetting to our modern sensibilities. How do we take what it says and apply it to our lives today? There has to be a simple and practical way to understand and apply the Bible that anyone can use.

This book is my attempt to help you. The main tool we will learn to use is a set of questions (that's the reason for the title!). The questions we ask when we read the Bible largely determine how we understand and apply it. So if we want to understand and apply the Bible, we need to make sure we are asking the right questions.

But how do we know which are the right questions to ask? Grasping what kind of book the Bible is, who and what it is about, and why God gave it to us is essential. That foundation sets us up to know what questions we should ask to understand the Bible.

If our goal is not just to understand but also to apply the Bible, then we also need to learn to read our lives the right way. As followers of Christ, we need to understand the basic pattern of the Christian life—turning away from sin (repentance) and trusting in who God is and what he has done for us (faith). From that starting point, we can then ask the key questions that enable us to apply the Bible to our lives.

That may seem like a lot of ground to cover in a short book. But by the end of this book you will be armed with four simple questions to help you understand the most important insights from any passage. You will also be armed with four simple questions to help you understand how to apply God's Word to your life so you can grow in your relationship with Jesus Christ. After all, as followers of Christ we should desire nothing more than to grow in our love for Christ and our obedience to him.

In fact, why not take a moment right now to pray that God will use this book to help you grow closer to him?

Ready? Let's get started with an overview of who and what the Bible is all about.

PART I

LAYING THE
FOUNDATION

1

The Story We Find Ourselves In

Everyone loves a good story. Whether it is kids begging for Dad to read them a book at bedtime or friends gathering to watch a movie, people enjoy hearing (and telling) stories. Think for a minute about the last time you caught up with an old friend you had not seen in a while. No doubt that conversation included a story or two.

But stories are for more than entertainment or providing information. They shape our understanding of who we are, why we exist, what kind of person we should be, and what kind of world we live in. Whether we realize it or not, we automatically connect everything we experience to what we believe to be the true story of the world. Our view of the world is inherently story shaped.

The Bible tells us the true story of the world, the way things truly are and should be. But because we are sinful, we are blind to this reality. Left to ourselves, we will default to understanding our lives within the false stories promoted by our culture or our own self-made stories. But when we are born again, the

Spirit of God opens our hearts and minds to understand what the Bible says about God, us, and the world around us. So if we are going to rightly understand who we are, why we exist, what kind of people we should be, and what kind of world we live in, the starting place is understanding the story of the Bible from Genesis to Revelation.

Now that can sound intimidating; after all, the Bible is a huge book! So in what follows I want to give you a brief overview of the story of the Bible. To help you remember the big picture, I have divided the story into six segments, each one beginning with the letter *c*: creation, crisis, covenants, Christ, church, and consummation.

Creation

The opening sentence of the Bible sets the stage for understanding the nature of the world around us: "In the beginning, God created the heavens and the earth" (Gen. 1:1). As the Creator, God has complete authority over all that exists. He has created the world to reflect his wisdom and beauty. Out of all that God has made, his masterpiece is humanity. Only human beings are said to be made in God's image. To make sure we don't miss this crucial point, the text says it four times in just two verses (Gen. 1:26–27)! God has created us as image bearers to reflect his character. We are made to be mirrors of his beauty and glory. What people think, believe, desire, and do should display who God is as we interact with him, each other, and creation.

As image bearers our first parents, Adam and Eve, are given a mission. God commands them to rule over creation under his authority, in essence making them kings (Gen. 1:28). God places them in the garden of Eden, which is his sanctuary on earth. They are to serve as priests in this sanctuary, maintaining its purity (Gen. 2:15–17). Through humanity God intends to mediate his presence to the world.

God has not designed us to live as isolated beings. He made us to experience community with each other. This is seen most clearly in the marriage relationship, where a man and a woman become one flesh (Gen. 2:18–25). But even aside from the marriage relationship, God has designed human beings to display his perfections more fully together than any one individual possibly could.

Crisis

The peaceful picture of Genesis 1–2 does not last long. God warned Adam and Eve that if they ate from the tree of the knowledge of good and evil, they would surely die (Gen. 2:15–17). But Satan, masquerading as a serpent, convinces Adam and Eve to rebel against God by eating from the tree of the knowledge of good and evil (Gen. 3:1–6). Instead of "being like God" as Satan promised, Adam and Eve experience the shame and guilt of disobeying their Creator (Gen. 3:7). Instead of harmony with God and each other, guilt and shame enter in. Instead of running to God, they try to hide from him (Gen. 3:8).

When God confronts them, he announces judgment. The Serpent is cursed to crawl and eat dust. But more importantly, God makes this promise to the Serpent (in the presence of Adam and Eve):

> I will put enmity between you and the woman,
>> and between your offspring and her offspring;
> he shall bruise your head,
>> and you shall bruise his heel. (Gen. 3:15)

In effect God is saying to the Serpent, "You may have defeated Adam and Eve, but there will come a day when a descendant of Eve will deal you a fatal blow. Yes, you will inflict a wound upon him, but in the end you will be crushed under his feet. My Serpent-crusher will ensure that I accomplish everything I have planned."

For Adam and Eve, judgment falls swiftly as well: increased pain in childbirth for the woman, as well a desire to undermine her husband's leadership in the marriage; increased difficulty in work for the man. Even creation itself is affected, as God places it under a curse. And when the time to die comes, human beings will return to the dust from which they were made.

Speaking of death, why don't Adam and Eve die immediately? Actually, they do—just not in the way we might expect. The ultimate kind of death is spiritual in nature; it is the kind of death that is the result of sin breaking a person's relationship with God. In the moment Adam and Eve rebel against God, they die spiritually. The physical death that follows hundreds of years later is simply the final outworking of their sin.

But judgment is not the final word for Adam and Eve. Although God has every right to end the whole program right there and destroy Adam and Eve for their rebellion, instead he shows mercy. God sacrifices some animals and uses their skins to clothe the man and the woman, which is symbolic of covering their sin (Gen. 3:21). But the damage to creation has been done. Their sin has opened the floodgates for death to ravage creation, leaving it a pale reflection of its original glory.

From that point forward, sin and death spread through creation like wildfire. Things eventually become so bad that God brings judgment in a massive flood that wipes out the entire human race, except Noah and his family (Genesis 6–9). But even though God scrubs the earth clean, the flood does not change the human heart or its inclination toward sin and evil. Not long after Noah and his family emerge from the ark, they too show themselves to be just like Adam by disobeying God's purpose to be fruitful, multiply, and fill the earth (Gen. 9:1). This rebellion culminates in the building of the Tower of Babel, where mankind unites to make a name for itself. God brings judgment and scatters the people into different languages (Gen. 11:1–9).

At this point things look grim, but God is just getting started.

Covenants

To bring the Serpent-crusher into the world, God makes a series of covenants. A covenant is a solemn commitment that God makes with a specific person or group of people to do and/or be something. As part of that commitment, God makes promises and places himself under an oath to fulfill them.

While there are hints of a covenant with Adam and a covenant that God makes with Noah (Gen. 6:18; 9:16–17), our starting point is with Abram (later renamed Abraham) and his barren wife Sarai (later renamed Sarah). Seemingly out of nowhere, God makes a stunning promise to them:

> Go from your country and your kindred and your father's house to the land that I will show you. And I will make of you a great nation, and I will bless you and make your name great, so that you will be a blessing. I will bless those who bless you, and him who dishonors you I will curse, and in you all the families of the earth shall be blessed. (Gen. 12:1–3)

Here God is revealing how he is going to bring about the promised Serpent-crusher. He will form Abraham into a great nation and bless all the nations of the earth through him. Through Abraham's line God will fulfill his plan of ruling over creation through humanity. Eventually Sarah gives birth to

Isaac as the promised son through whom God will continue the line of promise (Gen. 17:15–21; 21:1–7). God then renews the promise with Isaac's son Jacob (renamed Israel), and eventually with his twelve sons, from whom come the twelve tribes of Israel (Genesis 26–50).

Hundreds of years later Abraham's descendants have multiplied exponentially but find themselves enslaved in Egypt (Exodus 1). In response to their prayers for deliverance, God raises up Moses to deliver his people from Egypt (Exodus 2–6). Through Moses and his brother, Aaron, God brings a series of plagues on Egypt (Exodus 7–12), culminating in the death of the firstborn (marked by the celebration of Passover). Moses leads the Israelites out of Egypt, across the Red Sea, and to the foot of Mount Sinai (Exodus 13–19). When they arrive there, God meets with them. He instructs Moses to say to the people:

> You yourselves have seen what I did to the Egyptians, and how I bore you on eagles' wings and brought you to myself. Now therefore, if you will indeed obey my voice and keep my covenant, you shall be my treasured possession among all peoples, for all the earth is mine; and you shall be to me a kingdom of priests and a holy nation. These are the words that you shall speak to the people of Israel. (Ex. 19:4–6)

God is forming the descendants of Abraham into a nation. By describing them as a "kingdom of priests" God is assigning to Israel a modified version of the commission given to Adam and Eve. Whereas Adam and Eve were designated as priest-kings who ruled over creation from the garden of Eden, Israel is designated a kingdom of priests who will bless the nations from the land of Canaan. This covenant that God is making with the nation of Israel at Mount Sinai is the temporary means by which God will preserve the line of the promised Serpent-crusher and set his people apart from the other nations. As part of this covenant God gives Israel the law to teach them how to live as a kingdom of priests (Exodus 20–31).

But just like Adam and Eve, Israel blows it. Big time. Less than forty days after God spoke to Israel from Mount Sinai, Israel worships a golden calf (Exodus 32–34). Although God forgives them, this is but the first of many times when Israel goes after other gods. After wandering in the wilderness forty years (Numbers 13–36), they finally enter the Promised Land under the leadership of Joshua, Moses's successor (Joshua 1).

During the lifetime of Joshua, Israel manages to gain control of much of Canaan (Joshua 2–24). But pockets of resistance remain, and in the hundreds of years that follow, these surrounding peoples periodically oppress Israel (Judges 1–16). Such oppression is God's judgment for Israel's idolatry. When Israel cries out for deliverance, God raises up judges to rescue his people. This cycle repeats itself over and over again. Something has to change.

When Israel has finally had enough, the people ask God for a king (1 Samuel 8). They want to be just like the other nations. But that's just it—Israel is not supposed to be just like all the other nations! They are supposed to be a kingdom of priests, a holy nation set apart by God to display his character to the rest of the world. Nevertheless, God gives them a king. But he gives them the kind of king the nations have—a man named Saul who is tall, strong, handsome, and wealthy (1 Samuel 9–15). But he is not fully devoted to the Lord, and God eventually rejects Saul as his king.

In his place God anoints David (1 Sam. 16:1–13). As a man after God's heart, David becomes the standard by which every other king will be judged. Eventually God makes a stunning promise to David:

When your days are fulfilled and you lie down with your fathers, I will raise up your offspring after you, who shall come from your body, and I will establish his kingdom. He shall build a house for my name, and I will establish the throne of his kingdom forever. I will be to him a father, and he shall be to me a son. When he commits iniquity, I will discipline him with the rod of men, with the stripes of the sons of men, but my steadfast love will not depart from him, as I took it from Saul, whom I put away from before you. And your house and your kingdom shall be made sure forever before me. Your throne shall be established forever. (2 Sam. 7:12–16)

David is promised a descendant who will rule over an eternal kingdom and build a sanctuary for God to dwell with his people. God is making it clear that he is still pursuing his mission of ruling over creation through humanity for the display of his own glory. This promise finds initial and partial fulfillment in David's son Solomon, who extends his kingdom beyond the borders of Israel and builds a temple for the Lord to dwell in (1 Kings 1–10). But just as all before him, Solomon fails (1 Kings 11). He pursues the gods of his foreign wives. The nation begins to spiral downward, splitting into northern (Israel) and southern (Judah) kingdoms (1 Kings 12). It becomes so bad that God first sends Israel (2 Kings 17) and then Judah (2 Kings 25) into exile.

As the kingdoms of Israel and Judah continue their downward spiral into further idolatry, God raises up prophets to announce not only pending judgment but also the hope of restoration. Prophets such as Amos and Hosea announce the coming day of the Lord, when God will bring judgment on both his enemies and his rebellious people, but also redemption for the faithful remnant of his people. They foresee a day when a new people of God, consisting not merely of Jews but of Gentiles as well, will live under the rule of a Davidic King. God will transform not only his people but creation itself so that he may dwell with them forever.

Later prophets such as Isaiah, Jeremiah, and Ezekiel build on the prophecies of Amos and Hosea by announcing God's promise of a new covenant:

> Behold, the days are coming, declares the LORD, when I will make a new covenant with the house of Israel and the house of Judah, not like the covenant that I made with their fathers on the day when I took them by the hand to bring them out of the land of Egypt, my covenant that they broke, though I was their husband, declares the LORD. For this is the covenant that I will make with the house of Israel after those days, declares the LORD: I will put my law within them, and I will write it on their hearts. And I will be their God, and they shall be my people. And no longer shall each one teach his neighbor and each his brother, saying, "Know the LORD," for they shall all know me, from the least of them to the greatest, declares the LORD. For I will forgive their iniquity, and I will remember their sin no more. (Jer. 31:31–34)

> And I will give you a new heart, and a new spirit I will put within you. And I will remove the heart of stone from your flesh and give you a heart of flesh. And I will put my Spirit within you, and cause you to walk in my statutes and be careful to obey my rules. (Ezek. 36:26–27)

God will write his law directly on the hearts of his people. Full and final forgiveness will come. Cleansing from impurity and idolatry will be a reality. He will give his people a new heart and a new spirit to obey him. The Spirit of God will dwell in all of his people to empower their obedience. When this new covenant is established, there will be a people of God marked by a personal knowledge of the Lord based on final forgiveness of sins and expressed in greater heart-level obedience.

All of this will be accomplished through the One who is the Serpent-crusher, the Prophet greater than Moses, the Priest greater than Aaron, the conqueror greater than Joshua, David's greater son, the King wiser than Solomon, the servant of the Lord. He will obey where Adam, Noah, Israel, David, Solomon, and all the rest of humanity have failed. He will bring a new Spirit-empowered and Spirit-indwelt people of God into existence to live under his rule and authority in a new heaven and new earth. God will accomplish his purpose of ruling over creation through humanity.

But as the Old Testament closes, the question is When will the promised one come?

Christ

The New Testament begins by clearly identifying Jesus as the promised Serpent-crusher. He is the promised descendant of Abraham through whom God will bless all the nations (Matt. 1:1). He is the Son of David who will rule over an eternal kingdom. Unlike Adam, who failed in the garden, and Israel, who failed in the wilderness, Jesus defeats the Devil in the wilderness by refusing to give in to his temptations (Luke 4:1–13). He is the Spirit-anointed King who announces that the kingdom of God has arrived. Jesus calls for people to turn away from their sins and trust in him to be right with God (Mark 1:14–15).

To validate his message, Jesus begins performing miracles: healing the sick, casting out demons, calming a storm, feeding thousands of people with almost no food, and even raising people from the dead. Out of his growing number of followers, Jesus selects twelve men as apostles to be with him and to preach his message of the kingdom (Mark 3:13–19).

But as Jesus's popularity grows, so does opposition to him. The religious leaders begin to plot how to eliminate the threat that Jesus poses to their way of life. Meanwhile Jesus begins to tell his followers that he must suffer and die at the hands of the religious leaders but that three days later he will rise from the dead (Mark 8:31). Despite these clear predictions, the disciples simply cannot wrap their minds around the idea of a suffering Messiah.

Everything comes to a head when Jesus visits Jerusalem to celebrate the Passover. While there, he is arrested, beaten, and sentenced to be crucified as a political revolutionary (Mark 14–15). But what the Jewish leaders and Roman authorities mean for evil, God means for good. Not only does Jesus live a life of perfect obedience to God; he also willingly lays down his life as a sacrifice for sin. Through his death on the cross Jesus pays the penalty we deserve for our sinful rebellion against God.

The story doesn't end with Jesus's death, however. Three days later he rises from the dead, defeating sin, death, and the Devil himself (Luke 24). Jesus's resurrection shows definitively that God has begun to make all things new. The curse that fell upon creation when Adam rebelled is now being reversed! But it is not yet time for God to complete his plans of a new heaven and new earth. So Jesus spends forty days teaching his disciples about the kingdom of God and preparing them for their coming mission (Acts 1:1–11). But they must wait in Jerusalem until God sends the Holy Spirit to empower them for that mission. Jesus then ascends into heaven to sit at the right hand of the Father, awaiting the day when he will return for his people.

Church

Less than two weeks later—on the day of Pentecost—it happens: God pours out the Holy Spirit on the disciples (Acts 2:1–41). Peter preaches the good news about Jesus to the thousands of Jews gathered in Jerusalem from all across the Mediterranean world. In response three thousand people turn from their sin, trust in Jesus to have their sins forgiven, and are baptized. These new followers of Jesus form a new community, sharing a common life that shows they are the true people of God.

From these humble origins the church starts to spread. Beginning in Jerusalem the gospel expands throughout the Mediterranean world, led especially by the efforts of the apostle Paul (Acts 3–28). Through their self-sacrificial love and bold witness for Jesus, fledgling communities of faith become outposts of God's kingdom invading this fallen world.

And this is where we as the church find ourselves today. Jesus dwells in his people through the Holy Spirit to transform us and spread his kingdom to the ends of the earth. We are called to make disciples by sharing the good news of what Jesus has done and teaching people to obey what he has commanded (Matt. 28:18–20). Because we are joined to Christ by faith, we are "a chosen race, a royal priesthood, a holy nation, a people for his own possession," called to "proclaim the excellencies of him who called you out of darkness into his marvelous light" (1 Pet. 2:9).

We live out this mission as "sojourners and exiles" in this world, called to live in a way that will cause even unbelievers to glorify God (1 Pet. 2:11–12). We pursue lives of purity and holiness in anticipation of Christ's return (1 John 3:1–3). Even in the midst of our suffering, the Spirit empowers us to set our hope on the day when God will transform all creation for his glory and our good (Rom. 8:19–25).

Consummation

When the time finally comes for God to consummate all that he has promised, it will take our breath away. Christ will return in glory. God will usher in a new heaven and a new earth, where God will dwell with his people:

> And I heard a loud voice from the throne saying, "Behold, the dwelling place of God is with man. He will dwell with them, and they will be his people, and God himself will be with them as their God. He will wipe away every tear from their eyes, and death shall be no more, neither shall there be mourning, nor crying, nor pain anymore, for the former things have passed away." (Rev. 21:3–4)

> Then the angel showed me the river of the water of life, bright as crystal, flowing from the throne of God and of the Lamb through the middle of the street of the city; also, on either side of the river, the tree of life with its twelve kinds of fruit, yielding its fruit each month. The leaves of the tree were for the healing of the nations. No longer will there be anything accursed, but the throne of God and of the Lamb will be in it, and his servants will worship him. They will see his face, and his name will be on their foreheads. And night will be no more. They will need no light of lamp or sun, for the Lord God will be their light, and they will reign forever and ever. (Rev. 22:1–5)

Transformed creation. God dwelling with his people. The curse lifted. Sins forgiven. God's people serving him and worshiping him unhindered. God's glory filling the earth. Redeemed humanity reigning over creation forever and ever. This is our destiny as followers of Jesus.

• • •

That, in a nutshell, is the true story of the world. This reality should transform the way we think, what we desire, and what we do. It should shape how we relate to God and how we relate to others. Every aspect of our lives, including how we read and apply the Bible, must be governed by this grand story stretching from Genesis to Revelation.

But a story this grand, this sweeping, this all-encompassing, can seem so big that it overwhelms us. We can find ourselves asking how this story affects our lives, what our role in the true story of the world is, and how the Bible fits into this picture. So that is what we need to explore in our next chapter.

2

The Bible Is God's Tool
to Change Us

Children are born imitators. Think about it for a minute. Every kid growing up imitates someone he or she looks up to. My kids love sports, so I constantly hear them say things like "LeBron dribbles between the legs, crosses over, steps back for a three—*good!* What a shot by LeBron!"

The impulse to imitate does not stop once we reach adulthood. Even as adults, we tend to speak and act like the people we admire. We buy clothes so we can dress like our favorite celebrities. We use the phrases they use, maybe even pick up some of their gestures. Maybe we even style our hair to match someone we look up to.

Why is that? Why do we as human beings tend to imitate the people we admire? The short answer is that God wired us that way. God made us to resemble whomever or whatever we worship. That is a key element of what it means to be made in the image of God. Understanding this concept is so important that we need to take a closer look.

Let's start by going back to Genesis 1:26–27:

> Then God said, "Let us make man in our image, after our likeness. And let them have dominion over the fish of the sea and over the birds of the heavens and over the livestock and over all the earth and over every creeping thing that creeps on the earth."
>
> So God created man in his own image,
>   in the image of God he created him;
>   male and female he created them.

At least part of what it means to be made in God's image is to resemble and reflect his character in how we think, how we feel, how we speak, and what we do. In effect, God made us to be mirrors that reflect his beauty and glory to the world around us.

Because we are image bearers, God gave humanity a commission to live out: "And God blessed them. And God said to them, 'Be fruitful and multiply and fill the earth and subdue it, and have dominion over the fish of the sea and over the birds of the heavens and over every living thing that moves on the earth'" (Gen. 1:28). God made us human beings to reflect his beauty as we fill the earth and rule over it under the authority of the ultimate King—God himself. By worshiping God, humanity would reflect his character.

God's Image Marred

But as we saw in the last chapter, things went horribly wrong. Adam and Eve rejected their identity as image-bearing mirrors by rebelling against God. Instead of joyfully submitting to God, they placed themselves at the center of the universe (Genesis 3). In other words, they committed idolatry. That, at least, is how Paul describes it in Romans 1:21–23:

For although they knew God, they did not honor him as God or give thanks to him, but they became futile in their thinking, and their foolish hearts were darkened. Claiming to be wise, they became fools, and exchanged the glory of the immortal God for images resembling mortal man and birds and animals and creeping things.

This act of rebellion, however, did not change the fact that as human beings we resemble what we worship. For example, notice what Psalm 115:3–8 says:

Our God is in the heavens;
>   he does all that he pleases.

Their idols are silver and gold,
>   the work of human hands.
They have mouths, but do not speak;
>   eyes, but do not see.
They have ears, but do not hear;
>   noses, but do not smell.
They have hands, but do not feel;
>   feet, but do not walk;
>   and they do not make a sound in their throat.
Those who make them become like them;
>   so do all who trust in them.

The psalmist warns against the worship of idols because inevitably those who worship them become like them. Because idols are blind, deaf, and dumb, those who worship them become spiritually blind, deaf, and dumb (see also Ps. 135:15–18; Isa. 44:1–20).

Idolatry is such a big deal to God that he made it the subject of the first two of the Ten Commandments:

And God spoke all these words, saying,
>   "I am the LORD your God, who brought you out of the land of Egypt, out of the house of slavery.

"You shall have no other gods before me.

"You shall not make for yourself a carved image, or any likeness of anything that is in heaven above, or that is in the earth beneath, or that is in the water under the earth. You shall not bow down to them or serve them, for I the LORD your God am a jealous God, visiting the iniquity of the fathers on the children to the third and the fourth generation of those who hate me." (Ex. 20:1–5)

When we think of idolatry, we tend to think of ancient or primitive people bowing down to statues made of precious metals or stone. But idolatry is much broader than that. At the most basic level an idol is anyone or anything we love or cherish more than God himself. Idolatry, then, is a heart-level issue. Look at what God says to Ezekiel about the exiles in Babylon: "Son of man, these men have taken their idols into their hearts, and set the stumbling block of their iniquity before their faces" (Ezek. 14:3). God rebukes the leaders of Israel for setting their affections on the false gods of their Babylonian captors. They have been living double lives—seeking the Lord's counsel from the prophet while treasuring their false gods in their hearts.

Since idolatry is a heart issue, it includes attitudes, desires, and inclinations. Paul commands the Colossians to "put to death therefore what is earthly in you: sexual immorality, impurity, passion, evil desire, and covetousness, which is idolatry" (Col. 3:5). Understood this way, idolatry is the main problem Jesus exposes in the rich young man who asks him what he must do to have eternal life (Matt. 19:16–29). When Jesus challenges him to sell all he owns and give the money to the poor, the man goes away sad because he is unwilling to give up his true god—his wealth.

So because of Adam's rebellion against God in the garden, we enter this world with a deeply ingrained tendency toward idolatry. We are like the shopping cart with the bent wheel that constantly pulls the cart in the same direction. The way idolatry shows up varies from person to person. But no one is immune to it. Unless someone intervenes at the deepest level of our hearts and souls, we will pursue idolatry in some form or fashion.

God's Image Renewed

Praise the Lord, that is exactly what has happened! As the true and complete image of God, Jesus Christ lived the life of perfect obedience we could not live. He died the death we should have died for our sins. He rose from the dead three days later to defeat our greatest enemies: sin, death, and the Devil. Forty days later he ascended into heaven, and shortly afterward poured out the Holy Spirit on his people.

One of the main things the Holy Spirit does is make people spiritually alive. Because we are descendants of Adam, we enter the world blinded to God's glory (2 Cor. 4:4). But when the Holy Spirit makes us spiritually alive, he opens our spiritual eyes to see "the light of the knowledge of the glory of God in the face of Jesus Christ" (2 Cor. 4:6). As a result, we are transformed into true worshipers who worship God in spirit and truth (John 4:23–24).

As we worship the one true God in Jesus Christ, we become like him. The fundamental principle that we resemble what we worship has not changed. What has changed, though, is the object of our worship. Paul puts it this way: "And we all, with unveiled face, beholding the glory of the Lord, are being transformed into the same image from one degree of glory to another. For this comes from the Lord who is the Spirit" (2 Cor. 3:18).

We see the glory of the Lord as we see his character and actions. As we see who Christ is and what he has done for us, we are transformed so that we more fully reflect the image of Jesus Christ himself. The apostle John makes a similar point: "Beloved, we are God's children now, and what we will be has not yet appeared; but we know that when he appears we shall be like him, because we shall see him as he is. And everyone who thus hopes in him purifies himself as he is pure" (1 John 3:2–3).

Notice the progression. When Christ appears, we as his people will be like him, because we will see him as he truly he is. In other words, seeing Jesus face-to-face is what will complete the process of becoming a perfect reflection of Christ. Because this is our ultimate future hope, we purify ourselves in the present just as Jesus Christ is pure.

God has always demanded the wholehearted worship of his people. Look, for example, at Deuteronomy 6:4–5: "Hear, O Israel: The LORD our God, the LORD is one. You shall love the LORD your God with all your heart and with all your soul and with all your might." Because God is one, he deserves our complete devotion. This passage was known as the Shema because *shema* (meaning "hear") is its first word in Hebrew. It became so important to the Jewish people that by the time of Jesus, pious Jews would recite it every day. When asked what the greatest commandment was, Jesus responded by quoting this very verse (Matt. 22:35–40).

Jesus called his disciples to the same level of devotion. Explaining what it costs to follow him, he said: "If anyone would come after me, let him deny himself and take up his cross and follow me. For whoever would save his life will lose it, but whoever loses his life for my sake and the gospel's will save it" (Mark 8:34–35). God calls us to this kind of wholehearted devotion to him because he knows that he is what we need most and what will bring us our greatest joy. That is why David says:

One thing have I asked of the LORD,
   that will I seek after:
that I may dwell in the house of the LORD
   all the days of my life,
to gaze upon the beauty of the LORD
   and to inquire in his temple. (Ps. 27:4)

Oh, taste and see that the LORD is good!
   Blessed is the man who takes refuge in him! (Ps. 34:8)

As a deer pants for flowing streams,
   so pants my soul for you, O God.
My soul thirsts for God,
   for the living God.
When shall I come and appear before God? (Ps. 42:1–2)

O God, you are my God; earnestly I seek you;
   my soul thirsts for you;
my flesh faints for you,
   as in a dry and weary land where there is no water.
So I have looked upon you in the sanctuary,
   beholding your power and glory.
Because your steadfast love is better than life,
   my lips will praise you. (Ps. 63:1–3)

As we see the beauty of God in Jesus Christ, not only are we transformed to reflect his beauty; we also experience the joy that God designed us to experience.

God's Tool for Renewal: The Bible

So where do we see the beauty and glory of Jesus Christ most clearly? In the Bible. God has given us the Bible to tell us who he is, what he has done for us, and how we should live. He uses the Bible to change us so that our lives demonstrate that we bear his image. Psalm 1:2 says of the blessed person,

His delight is in the law of the LORD,
    and on his law he meditates day and night.

As a result of meditating on God's Word,

He is like a tree
    planted by streams of water
that yields its fruit in its season,
    and its leaf does not wither.
In all that he does, he prospers. (Ps. 1:3)

Psalm 19 is even clearer on the connection between hearing/reading/meditating on God's Word and God transforming us through it. After describing how the heavens declare the glory of God (19:1–6), David turns to the power of God's Word (19:7–11):

The law of the LORD is perfect,
    reviving the soul;
the testimony of the LORD is sure,
    making wise the simple;
the precepts of the LORD are right,
    rejoicing the heart;
the commandment of the LORD is pure,
    enlightening the eyes;
the fear of the LORD is clean,
    enduring forever;
the rules of the LORD are true,
    and righteous altogether.
More to be desired are they than gold,
    even much fine gold;
sweeter also than honey
    and drippings of the honeycomb.
Moreover, by them is your servant warned;
    in keeping them there is great reward.

Look at all the things that God's Word does: revives the soul, makes the simple wise, rejoices our hearts, enlightens our eyes, and warns us. No wonder David describes God's Word as more desirable than gold and sweeter than the sweetest honey!

Notice David's response to what God's Word is and what it does (19:12–14):

> Who can discern his errors?
>> Declare me innocent from hidden faults.
> Keep back your servant also from presumptuous sins;
>> let them not have dominion over me!
> Then I shall be blameless,
>> and innocent of great transgression.
>
> Let the words of my mouth and the meditation of
>> my heart
>> be acceptable in your sight,
> O LORD, my rock and my redeemer.

Reading God's Word reveals our sin to us and calls us to confess it and turn away from it. It prompts a desire in God's people to pursue spiritual growth so that what we say, think, do, and feel reflects the one who is our Rock and our Redeemer.

This transformation, however, does not take place in isolation. We hear, read, and study the Bible not only as individuals, but also as part of a community of fellow believers—the church. God has given us other Christians to learn from and learn with as we take in God's Word. As we hear the Word preached and taught, study it together in small groups, and talk about it with other believers, God uses his Word to transform us into clearer reflections of his Son, Jesus Christ.

• • •

So at the heart of application is the fundamental truth that we resemble what we worship. As a result, applying the Bible to our lives is first and foremost a reorientation of our whole lives to Christ, a commitment to see him for all his beauty and experience the transformation that comes from seeing his glory. The primary tool he uses to do this is the Bible.

If this is God's plan, then we need to make sure we are reading the Bible the right way. So how should we read the Bible? That's what we'll tackle in the next chapter.

PART 2

READING
THE BIBLE

3

Reading the Bible as Jesus Did

Reading the Bible can be intimidating. After all, it has sixty-six separate books and describes events that happened and people that existed thousands of years ago. Many of these people even have strange names that are impossible to pronounce. Sometimes the Bible uses words we do not understand. And sometimes it describes practices and rituals that are, quite frankly, bizarre to us as those who live in the modern world. (I'm looking at you, Leviticus.) No wonder many well-intentioned plans of reading the Bible end in frustration or disillusionment!

But what if the Bible itself has told us how it should be read? Or better yet—what if the One who inspired the Bible has given us guidelines on reading it? Seem too good to be true? Well it's not, because that is exactly what Jesus has done. So let's look first at what Jesus has to say about how to read the Bible, and then look at how he teaches his followers to read the Bible. Once we have done that, we can summarize four key principles to help us read the Bible as Jesus did.

John 5:39

Given the number of times the religious leaders argue with Jesus, it is not surprising that he clashes with them over how to read the Bible. After Jesus heals a man on the Sabbath (John 5:1–9), the Jewish leaders confront Jesus (5:10–46). Rather than back down, Jesus makes the situation even more tense! He further infuriates them by equating his work with what God the Father is doing (5:17). By calling God his Father, Jesus is "making himself equal with God" (5:18). He affirms that whatever the Father does, the Son also does, including raise the dead and execute judgment (5:19–29).

Because his claims are so staggering, Jesus brings forward witnesses to verify what he says (John 5:30–47). Not only does John the Baptist confirm Jesus's claims (5:32–35), but so do the works that the Father gives him to do (5:36). Despite the Jewish leaders' prominence, Jesus bluntly says that they have not heard God's voice, seen his form, or had his word abiding in them (5:37–38). Then Jesus makes this stunning statement: "You search the Scriptures because you think that in them you have eternal life; and it is they that bear witness about me, yet you refuse to come to me that you may have life" (5:39–40).

Stop for a minute to realize what Jesus is saying. These Jewish leaders, who have been considered the leading experts on the Old Testament, have missed the main point of the Scriptures—Jesus himself! The very people who should have most readily recognized who Jesus is based on their knowledge of the Bible not only have failed to recognized him as Messiah but also are actively opposing him.

Jesus concludes this encounter with sobering words for these Jewish leaders. On the last day, when these leaders appear before God, Jesus says:

Do not think that I will accuse you to the Father. There is one who accuses you: Moses, on whom you have set your hope. For if you believed Moses, you would believe me; for he wrote of me. But if you do not believe his writings, how will you believe my words? (John 5:45–47)

The very words of Moses that these Jewish leaders cherish will be the basis for their condemnation by God on the last day. And Moses will be one of the prosecuting attorneys.

From this passage we can draw at least two conclusions. First, Jesus believes that Scripture points to him in such a clear way that those who read Scripture should see him in its pages. In fact, he holds people responsible for not doing so, with eternal consequences.

Second, there are ways of reading Scripture that miss the main point of the Bible. That danger remains just as real today. So as followers of Jesus we must be sure we are reading the Bible the right way. Jesus addresses this issue even more directly in Luke 24.

Luke 24

Luke gives the most extended account of the day Jesus rose from the dead. After the discovery of the empty tomb by the women (24:1–12), the scene shifts to two of Jesus's followers walking on the road to Emmaus (24:13–35). As they discuss the events of the weekend, Jesus joins their conversation. Not realizing that it is Jesus (24:16 says, "Their eyes were kept from recognizing him"), the men begin to explain to him all that has happened. They describe Jesus as "a prophet mighty in deed and word before God and all the people" (24:19) who was condemned by the religious leaders and handed over to be crucified (24:20). Before these events they "had hoped that he was the one to redeem Israel" (24:21). But then the unexpected happened: some women discovered that Jesus's tomb was empty and were told by angels that he had risen from the dead (24:22–23). This seemingly unbelievable news was even confirmed by some of his male followers (24:24).

Rather than marvel at the events the men describe, Jesus sternly rebukes them: "O foolish ones, and slow of heart to believe all that the prophets have spoken! Was it not necessary that the Christ should suffer these things and enter into his glory?" (24:25–26). Far from being a tragic turn of events, all that happened in Jerusalem was absolutely necessary, Jesus insists. But he does not leave the two men wondering what he means by this; notice what he does next: "And beginning with Moses and all the Prophets, he interpreted to them in all the Scriptures the things concerning himself" (24:27).

Can you imagine being in on that "Bible study"? Jesus starts with the first five books of the Bible (written by Moses) and continues on through "all the Prophets." By "all the Prophets," Jesus means not just the books that today we call the prophetic books (Isaiah, Jeremiah, Ezekiel, Daniel, the twelve "Minor" Prophets) but also what we call the Historical Books (basically Joshua through 2 Kings). Jesus works his way through these books of the Bible, interpreting them so that these two men can understand how they point to him. The way Luke describes this event strongly suggests that Jesus is not merely highlighting individual verses or passages, but explaining how the whole storyline of the Old Testament points toward him.

Given how much space Luke devotes to this encounter, it is clear that he wants to emphasize the risen Jesus explaining how to read the Old Testament. And when Luke returns to this same subject later in this same chapter, any remaining doubt is removed. But first we need to set the stage.

It is later that night. The two men Jesus met on the road to

Emmaus have returned to Jerusalem and told the small band of Jesus's followers what happened to them when he appeared to them (Luke 24:33–35). As they are talking about this, Jesus appears in their midst (24:36). Despite their initial fear, Jesus reassures them of who he is, even going so far as to eat a piece of fish in front of them (24:37–43)!

With their fears now relieved, Jesus begins to piece together what happened, starting at the same place where he began with the two men on the road earlier that day: "These are my words that I spoke to you while I was still with you, that everything written about me in the Law of Moses and the Prophets and the Psalms must be fulfilled" (Luke 24:44). What Jesus has said to the two men on the road to Emmaus he now repeats to the larger group of disciples. In addition to mentioning again Moses and the Prophets, here Jesus also refers to the Psalms. By doing so Jesus is reinforcing his claim that the whole Old Testament finds its fulfillment in who he is and what he has done.

But without what happens next, Jesus's disciples will not get it. So, Luke says, Jesus "opened their minds to understand the Scriptures" (24:45). While this is no doubt a supernatural act, Jesus opens their minds by means of the explanation of the Scriptures that follows. Jesus says, "Thus it is written, that the Christ should suffer and on the third day rise from the dead, and that repentance and forgiveness of sins should be proclaimed in his name to all nations, beginning from Jerusalem" (24:46–47).

Normally when someone in the Bible says or writes, "It is written," he is about to quote a specific passage of Scripture. But that is not what Jesus does here. Instead, he provides a summary of the message of the Old Testament. According to Jesus, the basic message of the Old Testament has two main points: (1) the Christ would suffer and then rise from the dead, and

(2) repentance and forgiveness would be proclaimed to all the nations. Of these realities the disciples are "witnesses" (Luke 24:48). But Jesus does not leave his disciples on their own to live as witnesses. He instructs them to wait in Jerusalem "until you are clothed with power from on high" (24:49).

So what do we learn about reading the Bible from this passage? First, Jesus rebukes his followers for failing to recognize that *the main message of Scripture is focused on him.* Jesus expects his people to understand the Bible in a certain way. So if we read the Bible in a way that doesn't see Jesus and what he has done through the gospel as central, we are not reading the Bible the way Jesus tells us to read it.

Second, *reading and understanding the Bible the way Jesus commands requires help from God.* In both encounters, Luke makes it clear that Jesus enables his followers to read and understand the Old Testament the right way. Although this passage does not spell it out, the Holy Spirit is the one who does this work of illumination (1 Cor. 2:6–16). He is the one who enables us to understand God's Word.

Third, *all of Scripture points in some way to Christ and what he has done for us.* It's not just certain obvious passages that point to Christ and the gospel. Every single passage in some way points to the need for Christ, anticipates/describes who he is, anticipates/describes what he does, or indicates how we should live as his people. God is bringing to fulfillment all that he has promised to do in and through Jesus Christ.

Fourth, *the basic story of Scripture centers on the death and resurrection of Jesus, the announcement of that good news to all the nations, and the call for people to turn from their sins and trust in Christ.* Everything from Genesis to Revelation relates in some way to this basic message. Jesus expects us to read the Bible through that set of lenses.

Now with our foundation in place, we are ready to look at four key principles that help us read and understand the Bible the way Jesus tells us to.

Guiding Principles for Reading the Bible

While the Bible nowhere gives us a list of principles to guide how we read Scripture, the following principles are rooted in what the Bible says and what the biblical authors do. Not only *can* we read and understand the Bible the way the biblical authors did, but we *should*. These principles are a starting point.

First, since Christ is the fulfillment of God's promises in the Old Testament and the focal point of what he is doing in this world, *every passage of Scripture connects to Christ and his work in some way.* Paul writes that "all the promises of God find their Yes in him. That is why it is through him that we utter our Amen to God for his glory" (2 Cor. 1:20). In other words, every promise of God depends in some way on the person and work of Jesus for its fulfillment. So we can go to any passage in the Bible with the confidence that it somehow points to Christ and the redemption he accomplished.

Second, despite all its diversity, *the Bible tells an overarching story of God establishing his kingdom by saving his people through Jesus Christ and sending out his saved people to proclaim his glory to the ends of the earth.* Leviticus is very different from Isaiah, and Isaiah is very different from Proverbs, and Proverbs is very different from Acts. But they are all part of the larger story that runs from Genesis to Revelation, and each has a role to play in that unfolding story. Within this story there are points of continuity (things that do not change, like God's character) and discontinuity (things that do change, like cultural customs) that we need to pay attention to as well.

Third, *because God is sovereign, he has ordered human history so that earlier events, people, and institutions correspond to later events, people, and institutions.* For example, when the prophets point forward to the redemption that God will bring in the future, they often describe it in the language of a new exodus. The original exodus points forward to an even greater act of redemption that God promises. So when we read the Bible, we should look for these points of correspondence.

Fourth, *as we read the Bible and grow in our understanding of who Christ is and what he has done, we should constantly deepen our understanding of both the Bible and Jesus Christ.* The earliest followers of Jesus were continually going back to the Bible with their understanding of who Jesus is and seeing fresh things in Scripture about him. In turn those new insights into Scripture further deepened their understanding of who Jesus is and what he has done. This ongoing process was like a spiral that rotated between Christ and Scripture with each successive pass shedding further light on the others. Or, to put it differently, when the early Christians looked at Jesus, they did so through the lenses of the Old Testament, and when they looked at the Old Testament, they did so through the lenses of redemption in Christ. We should do the same.

• • •

As followers of Jesus, we should want to read the Bible the way Jesus and his earliest followers did. Not only is this an act of obedience; it is the way to see Jesus Christ more clearly so that we are changed to reflect him more clearly. If we approach every passage of Scripture with the expectation that it will somehow point us toward Christ, we will begin to see Scripture in a fresh way. But as we do this, it is crucial that we remember that although the Bible is written for us, it was not written to us. In the next chapter we will flesh out what that means.

4

Written for Us but Not to Us

Today most people have greater access to the Bible than at any other point in human history. Even those who do not own personal copies of Scripture can usually access it online with a few clicks or taps. Yet this easy access can have the downside of blinding us to an important truth about the Bible—it was not written to us.

Yes, you read that correctly. The Bible was not written to us. None of us are ancient Israelites following Moses through the wilderness. None of us are eighth-century (BC) Israelites living through the decline of the northern kingdom of Israel. None of us are Jews languishing in exile in Babylon, wondering if God has completely abandoned us. None of us are first-century (AD) Christians living in Rome, Philippi, or Ephesus. When we read the Bible, there is a sense in which we are reading someone else's mail.

But (and this is huge), the Bible is written *for* us. Isaiah 40:8 says,

> The grass withers, the flower fades,
> but the word of our God will stand forever.

God inspired the human authors of Scripture so that the very words they wrote were the words of God. So while the words of Isaiah were directed to the ancient Israelites in the eighth century (BC), God inspired those words as the means by which he would speak to his people well beyond those specific historical circumstances. Though the Bible was not written *to* us, it was written *for* us.

This distinction may seem rather picky. But it makes an enormous difference when it comes to understanding and applying the Bible correctly. So let's look at three passages that help us see this distinction and then illustrate why it matters.

Romans 15:4

Romans is Paul's longest and most complete explanation of the gospel message he preached. He repeatedly quotes from the Old Testament to explain the content and significance of the gospel. As he begins to wrap up the letter, Paul pleads with the Romans to go out of their way to bear with and encourage one another (15:1–2). In 15:3 he reminds them that Christ was the ultimate example of one who did not selfishly please himself. Instead, borrowing words from Psalm 69:9, Paul indicates that "the reproaches of those who reproached you fell on me." As the ultimate righteous sufferer, Jesus models how the Roman believers should love one another when they disagree on nonessential matters.

But instead of further explaining Jesus's suffering, Paul gives a window into his understanding of the Old Testament to explain why he has just quoted Psalm 69:9. He writes, "For whatever was written in former days was written for our instruction, that through endurance and through the encouragement of the Scriptures we might have hope" (Rom. 15:4). From this verse we learn at least three things about how believers should understand the Bible and apply it to our lives.

First, *the Bible was written for our instruction.* When Paul reads from Scripture, he is convinced that God has specific instruction for him with respect to what we should believe and how we should live. Also notice the pronoun Paul uses; he says that Scripture was written for *our* instruction. As Christians, we read Scripture as both individuals and as a community of believers. There is a communal aspect embedded within Paul's words here. So when we read the Bible, we should expect God to instruct us.

Second, *Scripture produces perseverance and encouragement.* As we read the Bible and apply it to our lives, God empowers us to continue to trust in Christ and his promises. Through his Holy Spirit, God uses Scripture to encourage us that he is with us and faithful to fulfill his promises to us (Rom. 15:4). In the next verse, Paul prays that "the God of endurance and encouragement" would enable them to live in harmony and therefore bring glory to God (15:5).

Third, *a key goal of reading the Bible is to produce hope.* In everyday English, the word *hope* often has a note of uncertainty. We might look at dark clouds in the sky and say, "I hope it doesn't rain tomorrow." But in Scripture, hope refers to our faith-fueled expectation that what God promises, he will do. Earlier, in Romans 8:23–25, Paul put it like this:

> And not only the creation, but we ourselves, who have the firstfruits of the Spirit, groan inwardly as we wait eagerly for adoption as sons, the redemption of our bodies. For in this hope we were saved. Now hope that is seen is not hope. For who hopes for what he sees? But if we hope for what we do not see, we wait for it with patience.

As we read the Bible, God deepens our hope in his faithfulness to fulfill his promises and enables us to press forward with perseverance and encouragement as we await that day.

So here in Romans 15 we see that Paul expects believers to read the Bible for instruction to foster our hope in the faithfulness of God; and as we do so, God uses Scripture to produce perseverance and encourage us as we follow Christ.

1 Corinthians 10:1–13

When Paul writes to the church at Corinth, they are facing challenges on a number of fronts. To address these challenges Paul uses a variety of tools, including the Old Testament. One key issue the Corinthians face is whether or not believers may/should eat meat that has been used as part of an offering to false gods. This common practice in Corinth raises difficult questions for Gentile Christians who are invited to eat with their pagan friends.

At the heart of Paul's lengthy response (1 Cor. 8:1–10:33), the apostle draws on Israel's exodus out of Egypt and selected events from their wilderness wandering (1 Cor. 10:1–13). He introduces these events as happening to "our fathers" (10:1), inviting all believers—regardless of their ethnicity—to think of the Israelites as their spiritual ancestors. These spiritual forefathers experienced a powerful redemption, baptism, and life-saving provision (10:1–4), yet God was so angry with most of them that they perished in the wilderness (10:5). The reason was that Israel was guilty of idolatry, sexual immorality, putting the Lord to the test, and grumbling against him (10:6–10).

Paul then explains why Israel's wilderness experiences are important: "Now these things happened to them as an example, but they were written down for our instruction, on whom the end of the ages has come" (10:11). Each of these events serves as an "example," a word that suggests that Israel's experiences foreshadow realities the church must face. God inspired Moses to write them not merely for the sake of the Israelites but also to instruct God's people today. Therefore believers should be on guard against arrogance and the very real danger of temptation (10:12–13).

Just as in Romans 15:4, Paul insists in 1 Corinthians 10:1–13 that Scripture was written for our instruction. In this fascinating passage we learn at least two additional insights for how we should read Scripture. First, *God orchestrated history in such a way that what he inspired the authors of Scripture to record serves as examples of how we as believers should or should not live*. God wants us to see in Scripture patterns of how he has acted in human history and how people have responded to him, both positively and negatively. These patterns should shape our view of God and how we should live today.

Second, *believers are described as people "on whom the end of the ages has come."* Through the life, death, and resurrection of Jesus, God's kingdom has broken into this fallen world. As believers we have experienced the initial fulfillment of God's promises, but we still await the full and final consummation of these promises. The final period of human history, sometimes called the latter days in the Bible, has begun with the work of Jesus. All along, God intended the events and people of Scripture to serve as examples for the church.

So here in 1 Corinthians 10 we see that Paul expects believers to read Scripture in such a way as to recognize examples from the people, events, and experiences recorded there to instruct us how to live in obedience to God. We do this because God intended Scripture all along to serve this role for his people.

1 Peter 1:10–12

Peter wrote his first letter to a group of Christians facing various trials in their efforts to walk faithfully with Christ. So Peter reminds them of what God has done for them in Christ, climaxing with a reference to "the salvation of your souls" (1 Pet. 1:3–9). Mentioning their salvation leads Peter to write this:

> Concerning this salvation, the prophets who prophesied about the grace that was to be yours searched and inquired carefully, inquiring what person or time the Spirit of Christ in them was indicating when he predicted the sufferings of Christ and the subsequent glories. It was revealed to them that they were serving not themselves but you, in the things that have now been announced to you through those who preached the good news to you by the Holy Spirit sent from heaven, things into which angels long to look. (1:10–12)

The salvation we experience as believers was foretold in the Old Testament by the prophets, whom God inspired to speak and write down his words. Notice what these prophets prophesied about: "the grace that was to be yours" (1:10)—in other words, the grace that believers would experience through their trust in Jesus Christ.

As these prophets wrestled with what the Spirit of Christ revealed to and through them, God was not merely giving a message for the original hearers/readers. Peter says that God "revealed to them that they were serving not themselves but you" (1:12). When God inspired these prophets, he intended those words to be read, understood, and applied by his people who lived long after the prophets died. As we read the Bible, we can be confident that God has something to say to us through the words of Scripture.

So even though the Bible was not written directly to us, it was most certainly written for us. We may not be ancient Israelites or first-century Philippians, but we are Christians. The Bible is our book, inspired by God to show us his glory and what it means to follow Christ.

So What?

At this point you may be wondering why this distinction—the Bible is not written to us but is written for us—matters. The reason is simple: without it we are likely to make mistakes when we read and apply the Bible.

Imagine you're reading Genesis 22, where God tells Abraham, "Take your son, your only son Isaac, whom you love, and go to the land of Moriah, and offer him there as a burnt offering on one of the mountains of which I shall tell you" (22:2). Intuitively we realize that we should not offer one of our own kids as a sacrifice. We're not Abraham. God did not say this *to* us, but he did say it *for* us.

But let's look at a harder example. In Matthew 19:16–29 a rich man comes to Jesus and asks what he must do to inherit eternal life. After the rich man claims he has kept all the commandments, Jesus tells him, "If you would be perfect, go, sell what you possess and give to the poor, and you will have treasure in heaven; and come, follow me" (19:21). If we think these words are spoken to us, then all believers must sell everything to follow Jesus. But if we recognize that these words were spoken *to* the rich young ruler and written down *for* us, we can understand and apply them rightly.

These two examples are enough to show why it matters that the Bible was written not to us but for us. So when it comes to understanding the Bible rightly, how can we make sure we recognize this distinction? What are some simple and practical ways to read and understand the Bible so we can apply it to our lives? That's what we will tackle in the next chapter.

5

Four Foundational Questions

Good reporters know how to ask thought-provoking questions. We have all seen politicians squirm when seasoned journalists ask them penetrating questions. Asking the right kinds of questions can often reveal something new about a person we think we know well.

When it comes to studying and applying the Bible, asking good questions is essential. In a very real sense, the quality of the questions you ask determines what you get out of the text and your ability to apply it to your life. But we need to make sure we are asking the right kinds of questions. We would laugh at someone reading *Sports Illustrated* and asking what Shakespeare thought of women or looking for tips to get a child to eat lima beans. So when it comes to studying and applying the Bible, we need to ask not only good questions but also the kind of questions the Bible is designed to answer.

So what kind of questions is the Bible intended to answer? We have already seen that the Bible is first and foremost a story about God displaying his glory through the creation and redemption of humanity. It makes sense, then, that the Bible is designed to answer questions connected to this central theme. Jesus confirms this dual focus on God and humanity. When asked what the greatest commandment is, he replies, "You shall love the Lord your God with all your heart and with all your soul and with all your mind" (Matt. 22:37). But Jesus isn't done. He continues, "And a second is like it: You shall love your neighbor as yourself" (Matt. 22:39). Love God. Love others. This is the heart of what God wants from his people.

The challenge, then, is to ask questions that help us see these realities when we read the Bible. If that seems overwhelming, don't worry! By asking four foundational questions, we can make sure we are asking the kind of questions that God designed the Bible to answer.

What Do We Learn about God?

God is the main character of the Bible, the hero of the story. So it makes sense that the first question we ask is what we learn about him. Scripture reveals who God is in at least three different ways.

First, it shows us God's *character*, or his attributes. Sometimes the Bible states these directly. In Revelation 4:8 we learn that the four living creatures around God's throne cry out nonstop,

> Holy, holy, holy, is the Lord God Almighty,
>   who was and is and is to come!

It takes little effort to see from this passage that God is holy, all powerful, and eternal.

In other passages, however, what we learn about God must be inferred from what the text says. In 1 Kings 22:1–40, King Ahab of Israel rejects the word of the Lord and goes to battle with the king of Syria. The prophet Micaiah has warned him that he will die in battle, so Ahab disguises himself as a common soldier. Yet even the "random" release of an arrow reveals God's sovereign control: "But a certain man drew his bow at random and struck the king of Israel between the scale armor and the breastplate" (22:34).

Second, Scripture reveals who God is by showing us his *conduct*. In other words, we see God doing things in a passage that show us who he is. Psalm 23 is an excellent example:

> The LORD is my shepherd; I shall not want.
>> He makes me lie down in green pastures.
> He leads me beside still waters.
>> He restores my soul.
> He leads me in paths of righteousness
>> for his name's sake.
>
> Even though I walk through the valley of the
>> shadow of death,
>> I will fear no evil,
> for you are with me;
>> your rod and your staff,
>> they comfort me.
>
> You prepare a table before me
>> in the presence of my enemies;
> you anoint my head with oil;
>> my cup overflows.
> Surely goodness and mercy shall follow me
>> all the days of my life,
> and I shall dwell in the house of the LORD
>> forever.

Look at all the different things God does for his people: leads, restores, comforts, prepares, anoints. Paying attention to what

God is doing in a passage helps us grow in our understanding of God.

Third, the Bible reveals who God is by showing us his *concerns*. In Exodus 22:21–22, God commands his people, "You shall not wrong a sojourner or oppress him, for you were sojourners in the land of Egypt. You shall not mistreat any widow or fatherless child." God makes it clear that he values and protects the marginalized, and expects his people to do the same. Because God values them as image bearers, God's people should treat them with dignity and respect.

Character, conduct, and concerns. These are three different angles to help us see what a passage tells us about God. Distinguishing whether something shows God's character, his conduct, or his concerns is not the important thing; recognizing what the text teaches us about God is what matters.

When asking what we learn about God, we should be sure to pay attention to all three persons of the Trinity. In 2 Corinthians 13:14, Paul writes, "The grace of the Lord Jesus Christ and the love of God and the fellowship of the Holy Spirit be with you all." Here we see something true about each person of the Trinity. God the Father shows us love, the Lord Jesus Christ shows us grace, and we experience fellowship with the Holy Spirit.

Starting with what a passage teaches us about God reminds us that first and foremost the Bible is about him, not us. Once that building block is in place, we are ready to ask our second foundational question.

What Do We Learn about People?

As the pinnacle of God's creation, human beings are at the center of God's purposes for creation. He made us in his image to reflect his beauty and rule over creation under his loving authority (Gen. 1:26–31). But Adam and Eve rebelled against

God, and as their descendants, every single one of us enters the world as sinners (Genesis 3; Rom. 5:12–21). Those who have turned from their sin and trusted in Jesus Christ have been made spiritually alive and given the Holy Spirit but still must fight against sin (Rom. 8:12–13; 2 Cor. 5:17).

When it comes to learning what a passage teaches us about people, we can approach that from three different angles. The first angle is looking in the text for aspects of what it means to be *created* in the image of God. What longings or desires does the passage reveal that are expressions of being made in God's image? For example, Hannah, the barren wife of Elkanah, prays,

> O LORD of hosts, if you will indeed look on the affliction of your servant and remember me and not forget your servant, but will give to your servant a son, then I will give him to the LORD all the days of his life, and no razor shall touch his head. (1 Sam. 1:11)

God made us as human beings to be fruitful, multiply, and fill the earth (Gen. 1:28), so Hannah's desire to have a child is both natural and understandable.

Of course, sin regularly distorts our God-given desires and twists them in harmful directions and expressions. So the second angle to discover what a passage reveals about humanity is to look for the *fallen condition(s)* it exposes. I'll have much more to say about this in chapter 7. For now, we can simply describe the fallen condition as the sinful beliefs, attitudes, feelings, actions, or tendencies mentioned or implied in the text. In some passages the fallen condition is impossible to miss. Take, for example, Proverbs 6:16–19:

> There are six things that the LORD hates,
>   seven that are an abomination to him:

haughty eyes, a lying tongue,
    and hands that shed innocent blood,
a heart that devises wicked plans,
    feet that make haste to run to evil,
a false witness who breathes out lies,
    and one who sows discord among brothers.

In other texts, you may have to read between the lines to see the fallen condition. After hundreds of years of being led by judges, Israel asked the prophet Samuel to appoint a king for them (1 Sam. 8:1–9). Despite the Lord's warning about what a king would do (1 Sam. 8:10–18), the people insisted, saying, "No! But there shall be a king over us, that we also may be like all the nations, and that our king may judge us and go out before us and fight our battles" (1 Sam. 8:19–20).

The problem is that God never intended his people to be "like all the nations"; he called his people to be "a kingdom of priests and a holy nation" (Ex. 19:6). Thus the fallen condition here is rejecting our identity as the people of God, set apart for his special purposes in this world.

The third angle to get at what a passage reveals about people is to look for what our lives should look like as *redeemed* people. In Acts 2:42–47, Luke describes how the earliest believers lived out their faith in Jesus:

And they devoted themselves to the apostles' teaching and the fellowship, to the breaking of bread and the prayers. And awe came upon every soul, and many wonders and signs were being done through the apostles. And all who believed were together and had all things in common. And they were selling their possessions and belongings and distributing the proceeds to all, as any had need. And day by day, attending the temple together and breaking bread in their homes, they received their food with glad and generous hearts, praising God and having favor with all the people. And the Lord added to their number day by day those who were being saved.

This snapshot helps us see how the gospel transforms people to live as redeemed individuals, as well as a redeemed community.

Created, fallen, and redeemed. Each of these sheds light on what the Bible teaches us about humanity. Now we are ready to ask our third foundational question.

What Do We Learn about Relating to God?

Loving God with our whole being expresses itself in a variety of ways. So when we read the Bible, we want to pay attention to how we should relate to God. A good starting point is to consider three common ways we should respond to who God is and who we are.

The first is considering what we should *praise* God for. Take, for example, 1 Peter 1:3–5, where the apostle writes:

Blessed be the God and Father of our Lord Jesus Christ! According to his great mercy, he has caused us to be born again to a living hope through the resurrection of Jesus Christ from the dead, to an inheritance that is imperishable, undefiled, and unfading, kept in heaven for you, who by God's power are being guarded through faith for a salvation ready to be revealed in the last time.

Peter lists in rapid-fire fashion a number of things about what God has done for us in Christ and the benefits we receive from it: we are born again; we have a living hope; we have an inheritance; we are guarded by God's power. All of these are reasons to praise him.

Second, we should also ask what sin we need to *confess* and *repent* of. Confession means agreeing with God about our sin and acknowledging it to him. Repentance is turning away from our sin and taking tangible steps to pursue change in our lives. Confession and repentance do not earn us favor before God. Based on what Jesus has done, we have already been declared not guilty before God. But sin does break our fellowship with God, causing what we might call "relational distance." Confession and repentance are, together, the way we restore our fellowship with God. Since we have already identified the fallen condition of a passage (see above), we need to confess the specific ways it shows up in our own life. So returning to Proverbs 6:16–19, we want to recognize and then confess specific instances of haughty eyes, a lying tongue, and other sins that the Holy Spirit calls to mind. Again, I'll have more to say about this when we look further at our fallen condition in chapter 7.

Finally, we should ask what gospel promises we need to *believe*. This question helps us get at what we will call the gospel solution, which we will explore more fully in chapter 8. For now, we can describe it simply as aspects of the gospel mentioned in the passage that address the fallen condition we have already identified. Here's a good example from Ephesians 4:22–24, where Paul commands believers

> to put off your old self, which belongs to your former manner of life and is corrupt through deceitful desires, and to be renewed in the spirit of your minds, and to put on the new self, created after the likeness of God in true righteousness and holiness.

The gospel addresses the "deceitful desires" we must still fight against as Christians by renewing our minds to think in a way that honors Christ. Through the gospel God has begun to transform us into the "the likeness of God" so that we are no longer slaves to the deceitful desires that often feel so powerful in our experience. These are promises we need to believe to deepen our relationship with God.

Praise, confess and repent, and believe. These are several key ways we express our love for God. Now it's time to look at our fourth and final foundational question.

What Do We Learn about Relating to Others?

God created us to be in community with one another. When he saves us from our sins, he makes us part of the body of Christ. Jesus commands us to love our neighbor as ourselves. So let's consider what this looks like from three different perspectives.

First, consider what the passage teaches about living and *interacting* rightly with others. On a daily basis we interact with a variety of different people—family, friends, room-mates, coworkers, classmates, neighbors, fellow believers, non-Christians, and so on. The Bible has a lot to say about how we should relate to those around us. First Peter is a great example. The apostle writes, "Keep your conduct among the Gentiles honorable, so that when they speak against you as evildoers, they may see your good deeds and glorify God on the day of visitation" (2:12). Believers are instructed: "Honor everyone. Love the brotherhood. Fear God. Honor the emperor" (2:17). Servants should submit themselves to their master (2:18–25). Wives should submit to their husbands (3:1–6). Husbands must "live with [their] wives in an understanding way" (3:7). Christians should "have unity of mind, sympathy, brotherly love, a tender heart, and a humble mind" (3:8), refusing to pay back evil for evil (3:9–12). When unbelievers ask us why we are different from the world, we must be ready to give an answer (3:13–17). Following Jesus requires us to interact wisely with those around us. The Bible is the place for us to learn how to do that.

A second helpful angle is to consider what the passage teaches about *reconciling* with other people. Conflict in a fallen world is inevitable. As Christians we are called to "live peaceably with all," if possible (Rom. 12:18). Paul sharply rebukes the Corinthians for using the courts to resolve their conflicts rather than deal with them in the church (1 Cor. 6:1–11). He calls out two women in the church at Philippi to settle their differences, even asking others to get involved to help them, before they damage the church (Phil. 4:2–3).

Lastly, reflect on what the passage teaches about *loving, serving, and caring for others*. Second Samuel 9:1–13 tells the story of David summoning Mephibosheth to appear before him. As a grandson of Saul, the previous king, Mephibosheth likely expects to be executed, since ancient kings often eliminated any potential rivals to their thrones. Yet instead of killing him, David shows him kindness. He restores the family land to Mephibosheth and even invites him to eat at David's table like one of his own sons. What a beautiful picture of what it means to love and serve others well!

Interact, reconcile, and serve. These are just three common ways the Bible challenges us to love our neighbor as ourselves.

• • •

Now that we have explored each of the four foundational questions, let's step back for a minute to look at the big picture. Remember, the ultimate goal of reading the Bible is to have our lives transformed by God so we resemble our Lord Jesus. Asking these four foundational questions focuses our attention on the main message of the Bible and prepares us to apply biblical truths to our lives in meaningful ways.

So why not give it a try? Pick a chapter of the Bible and read through it, asking the four questions. Not sure where to start? Try Matthew 8. If you are a note taker, grab paper and a pen, or open a file to jot down what you learn for each question. Ask the Lord to open your eyes to see who he is, who you are, and what it means to walk with him faithfully.

PART 3

READING
OUR LIVES

6

The Gospel Pattern of Life

To one degree or another, we are all creatures of habit. Even if you think of yourself as a spontaneous person, you still live in a world that operates on certain set patterns. The most obvious is creation. The earth completes a full rotation every twenty-four hours, establishing the pattern of day and night. Every 365 days the earth also completes a lap around the sun, regulating the seasons. The moon rotates around the earth approximately every thirty days, controlling the tides of the oceans. God created the world with set patterns that regulate how it works.

Everyday life also has patterns. The hours we work often follow a set pattern. If you are a student or teacher, your pattern of life is in large part set by when school is in session, what time your classes meet, and when assignments are due. Family responsibilities also set patterns for us, such as preparing meals, cleaning the house, or taking care of the yard. Even our bodies establish patterns for us. The most obvious ones involve things like sleep and food. But even the cells in different parts of our body replace themselves on a regular schedule. We live in a world that functions on the basis of patterns.

It makes sense, then, that the Christian life also functions according to a pattern. I'm not talking about attending church, reading your Bible, praying, giving, or sharing the gospel. Those are all crucial aspects of living the Christian life, and they often establish rhythms or patterns in our lives. But I am talking about an even more fundamental pattern that is the heartbeat of the Christian life.

At the center of the Christian life is a pattern of repentance and faith. They are not only the entry point into the Christian life. They are also the ongoing pattern of the Christian life. But before we can see this pattern at work, we need to make sure we understand what the Bible means when it refers to repentance and faith.

A Biblical Understanding of Repentance and Faith

Discussing repentance and faith together is important because they are two sides of one coin. Let's start with repentance. At its most basic level, repentance is turning our lives away from sin. Joel 2:12–13 gives a good description of it:

> "Yet even now," declares the LORD,
>> "return to me with all your heart,
> with fasting, with weeping, and with mourning;
>> and rend your hearts and not your garments."
> Return to the LORD your God,
>> for he is gracious and merciful,
> slow to anger, and abounding in steadfast love;
>> and he relents over disaster.

Isaiah 55:6–7 offers another helpful description:

Seek the LORD while he may be found;
   call upon him while he is near;
let the wicked forsake his way,
   and the unrighteous man his thoughts;
let him return to the LORD, that he may have
      compassion on him,
   and to our God, for he will abundantly pardon.

Although turning away from our sin is something we must do, repentance is mysteriously described as a gift that God gives.

God exalted [Jesus] at his right hand as Leader and Savior, to give repentance to Israel and forgiveness of sins. (Acts 5:31)

And the Lord's servant must not be quarrelsome but kind to everyone, able to teach, patiently enduring evil, correcting his opponents with gentleness. God may perhaps grant them repentance leading to a knowledge of the truth, and they may come to their senses and escape from the snare of the devil, after being captured by him to do his will. (2 Tim. 2:24–26)

Repentance is more than simply changing your mind about sin. Genuine repentance produces tangible change in how we think, what we believe, what we desire, and how we act. Summarizing his preaching for King Agrippa, the apostle Paul says that he "declared first to those in Damascus, then in Jerusalem and throughout all the region of Judea, and also to the Gentiles, that they should repent and turn to God, performing deeds in keeping with their repentance" (Acts 26:20).

So to sum up, repentance is a gift from God that enables us to turn our whole lives away from sin to such a degree that it changes how we think, believe, feel, and act.

If repentance is turning away from sin, faith is turning

toward God. It is the commitment of our whole being to God. The Bible uses words like *believe*, *trust*, *commit*, and *delight* to describe it:

> Now faith is the assurance of things hoped for, the conviction of things not seen. For by it the people of old received their commendation. . . . And without faith it is impossible to please him, for whoever would draw near to God must believe that he exists and that he rewards those who seek him. (Heb. 11:1–2, 6)

> Trust in the LORD with all your heart,
>   and do not lean on your own understanding.
> In all your ways acknowledge him,
>   and he will make straight your paths. (Prov. 3:5–6)

> Trust in the LORD, and do good;
>   dwell in the land and befriend faithfulness.
> Delight yourself in the LORD,
>   and he will give you the desires of your heart.

> Commit your way to the LORD;
>   trust in him, and he will act. (Ps. 37:3–5)

We have already seen that repentance is a gift from God. The same is true of faith as well.

> For it has been granted to you that for the sake of Christ you should not only believe in him but also suffer for his sake (Phil. 1:29)

> Simon Peter, a bond-servant and apostle of Jesus Christ,

> To those who have received a faith of the same kind as ours, by the righteousness of our God and Savior, Jesus Christ (2 Pet. 1:1 NASB)

So faith is the gift of God that enables us to turn toward God in trust that he is who the Bible says he is and he has done what the Bible says he has done. This kind of genuine faith produces tangible acts of obedience.

Together, then, repentance and faith are two sides of the same coin. Repentance is turning away from our sin and faith is turning toward God in trust. They go hand in hand with each other. Together they are the basic pattern of the Christian life from start to finish.

Repentance and Faith: The Entry Point into the Christian Life

When the Holy Spirit makes us spiritually alive (John 3:1–8; Titus 3:3–7), we respond by repenting and believing. Consider Jesus's first words when he launches his public ministry: "The time is fulfilled, and the kingdom of God is at hand; repent and believe in the gospel" (Mark 1:15). The kingdom of God has arrived because Jesus the King has come. So the correct response to this good news is to turn away from sin (repent) and trust in Jesus as the one who forgives sin (faith).

This emphasis on repentance and faith is not unique to Jesus. When Paul meets with the elders from the church in Ephesus, he reminds them what his ministry is like (Acts 20:18–38). The apostle claims, "I did not shrink from declaring to you anything that was profitable, and teaching you in public and from house to house, testifying both to Jews and to Greeks of repentance toward God and of faith in our Lord Jesus Christ" (Acts 20:20–21). The centerpiece of Paul's ministry, regardless of the place or audience, is calling people to turn away from their sins and put their trust in Jesus Christ. Notice how he describes what God has accomplished through the preaching of the gospel in Thessalonica:

> For not only has the word of the Lord sounded forth from
> you in Macedonia and Achaia, but your faith in God has
> gone forth everywhere, so that we need not say anything.
> For they themselves report concerning us the kind of recep-
> tion we had among you, and how you turned to God from
> idols to serve the living and true God, and to wait for his
> Son from heaven, whom he raised from the dead, Jesus who
> delivers us from the wrath to come. (1 Thess. 1:8–10)

When the Thessalonians heard the gospel message, they turned
away from worshiping idols and turned toward God by trusting
in his Son Jesus Christ.

That is the experience of every believer. By definition a
Christian is someone who has turned from sin and put his or
her faith in Jesus Christ to be made right with God. Repentance
and faith are the entry point into the Christian life.

Repentance and Faith: The Pattern for the Christian Life

But repentance and faith are not just the entry point. They are
also the pattern of how we live the Christian life. In Ephesians
4:17–19, Paul calls believers to turn away from the sinful ways of
their lives before they knew Christ. The reason they must do so is
that the gospel establishes a pattern for the life of the Christian.

> But that is not the way you learned Christ!—assuming that
> you have heard about him and were taught in him, as the
> truth is in Jesus, to put off your old self, which belongs to
> your former manner of life and is corrupt through deceitful
> desires, and to be renewed in the spirit of your minds, and
> to put on the new self, created after the likeness of God in
> true righteousness and holiness. (Eph. 4:20–24)

By "learn[ing] Christ" Paul means hearing and respond-
ing to the gospel message about Christ, as the next phrase

("assuming that you have heard about him and were taught in him") makes clear. The content of that message is summarized as (1) "put off your old self," (2) "be renewed in the spirit of your minds," and (3) "put on the new self." Let's look at each of these more closely.

When Paul speaks of the old self, he means the sinful thoughts, beliefs, feelings, actions, desires, and so forth that characterize a person who does not know Christ. That "former manner of life . . . is corrupt through deceitful desires." To "put off" those things means to take them off like dirty clothes. In other words, it means to repent.

Because our minds are futile, because our hearts are hardened, and because our passions are self-centered, we will never repent and believe on our own. God must first, by his Spirit, renew us at the core of our being. He must breathe spiritual life into our deadness. He must shine light into our darkened and futile minds. He must replace our stony hard hearts with hearts of flesh that are sensitive to him. He must change our self-centered passions into a God-centered passion that overflows into the lives of others. Our condition apart from Christ is so desperate, so hopeless, that changing us requires the very same divine power that spoke the universe into existence (2 Cor. 4:6). That is how much we need to be transformed.

The final component of the message is to put on the new self. God calls us to put on a new identity, like a new set of clothes, as followers of Christ. This identity is "created after the likeness of God in true righteousness and holiness." Just as sin has corrupted every area of our lives, the obedience of Jesus Christ has covered every area of our lives. He has done everything necessary to earn us favor before a holy and righteous God. That is what Paul means here when he talks about putting on the new man. The good news of the gospel is that God gives us new clothes made of the perfect righteousness and holiness of his Son Jesus Christ. We receive those new clothes through our trust in Christ and his promises.

Paul applies the pattern of repentance and faith that began the Christian life to our ongoing experience of the Christian life. Immediately after summarizing this basic pattern of the gospel (Eph. 4:20–24), Paul writes, "Therefore, having put away falsehood, let each one of you speak the truth with his neighbor, for we are members one of another" (Eph. 4:25). The "therefore" that begins this verse signals that Paul expects believers to apply this gospel pattern of repentance and faith to the issues that follow. As believers read these commands describing what the Christian life looks like in practical terms, God exposes our sin so that we can turn from it and trust in his promises.

• • •

From start to finish, repentance and faith are the basic pattern of the Christian life. As we read the Bible, the Holy Spirit takes God's Word and uses it to transform us. But what practical steps can we take to identify areas where we need to repent? And how can we identify areas where we need to believe the gospel and apply it to our lives? That is where the next two chapters on our fallen condition and the gospel solution come in.

7

The Fallen Condition

We live in a fallen world. Just browsing the news headlines reminds us that evil is actively at work in the world. Another terrorist attack injures or kills hundreds. A new disease begins to spread rapidly, endangering entire countries. Brutal dictators continue to oppress their people. Wealthy corporations break the rules to maximize their profits and get away with it. Politicians lie and manipulate the system to increase their power.

We see the same kind of evil at work closer to home. A coworker bends the rules and gets the promotion you think you deserved. Your neighbors flaunt their immoral lifestyle. A close friend betrays your confidence. A loved one is diagnosed with a rare form of cancer that cannot be cured.

But evil and suffering are not limited to the world around us or even to our immediate circumstances and relationships. We can see it in our own lives. Not only do others sin against us, but we sin against God and others. Sinful desires tug at our hearts and minds, luring us to disobey God. Sinful words come out of our mouths and hurt others. Sinful actions come naturally to us.

Although the specific examples vary from person to person, the Bible is very clear that everyone sins. Here are just a few of the many clear statements the Bible makes on this subject:

> The heart is deceitful above all things,
>> and desperately sick;
>> who can understand it? (Jer. 17:9)

> . . . for all have sinned and fall short of the glory of God. (Rom. 3:23)

> Therefore, just as sin came into the world through one man, and death through sin, and so death spread to all men because all sinned . . . (Rom. 5:12)

> But the Scripture imprisoned everything under sin, so that the promise by faith in Jesus Christ might be given to those who believe. (Gal. 3:22)

> If we say we have no sin, we deceive ourselves, and the truth is not in us. (1 John 1:8)

Since one of the main reasons God gave us the Bible is to transform us to reflect his Son, Jesus Christ, it makes sense that Scripture reveals our sinfulness. Look at how Hebrews 4:12–13 describes it:

> For the word of God is living and active, sharper than any two-edged sword, piercing to the division of soul and of spirit, of joints and of marrow, and discerning the thoughts and intentions of the heart. And no creature is hidden from his sight, but all are naked and exposed to the eyes of him to whom we must give account.

When God's Word goes to work in our lives, it penetrates to the core of our being. It reveals our thoughts, intentions, motivations, desires, and inclinations. In other words, the Bible exposes our fallen condition.

What Is the Fallen Condition?

What exactly do we mean by fallen condition? Pastor Bryan Chapell offers this helpful definition: "The Fallen Condition Focus (FCF) is the mutual human condition that contemporary believers share with those to or about whom the text was written that requires the grace of the passage for God's people to glorify and enjoy him."[1] Even though the people to whom and about whom the Bible was written lived thousands of years before us, they were fallen human beings just like us. They lived in a fallen world just like we do. They experienced the same kinds of temptations, struggles, and hardships we face today.

The way the fallen condition shows up in our lives, however, can look quite different. In Luke 12:15–21, Jesus told this parable:

> And he said to them, "Take care, and be on your guard against all covetousness, for one's life does not consist in the abundance of his possessions." And he told them a parable, saying, "The land of a rich man produced plentifully, and he thought to himself, 'What shall I do, for I have nowhere to store my crops?' And he said, 'I will do this: I will tear down my barns and build larger ones, and there I will store all my grain and my goods. And I will say to my soul, "Soul, you have ample goods laid up for many years; relax, eat, drink, be merry."' But God said to him, 'Fool! This night your soul is required of you, and the things you have prepared, whose will they be?' So is the one who lays up treasure for himself and is not rich toward God."

---

1. Bryan Chapell, *Christ-Centered Preaching: Redeeming the Expository Sermon*, 2nd ed. (Grand Rapids, MI: Baker, 2005), 90.

An obvious fallen condition would look something like this: we seek to find life, joy, fulfillment, contentment, and/or security in the abundance of our possessions. But this fallen condition can show up in a variety of ways.

For the wealthy person, it may reveal itself in the arrogant assumption that all she has is the product of her own hard work and has nothing to do with God's kindness.

For the poor person, it may reveal itself in the constant preoccupation with acquiring more money/possessions, and the belief that if only he had a little more wealth, that would solve the vast majority of his problems.

Regardless of a person's wealth, the fallen condition may reveal itself in working long hours at the expense of time with family, supposing that life is found in providing a certain standard of living.

It may reveal itself in a person who turns to shopping to deal with the difficulties or frustrations of life, believing that buying one more thing will bring joy.

It may reveal itself in a person who is stingy and refuses to give generously, fearing that if too much is given away, his or her desired lifestyle will suffer.

In the retiree, it may show itself in an attitude that views the retirement years as an entitlement to be lazy or selfish in how time and resources are spent. After all, years of hard work now entitle me to spend my time and energy on whatever I want.

As you can see, then, the fallen condition identified in a passage can reveal itself in different ways depending on a person's circumstances, personality, upbringing, culture, and more. If you are not a wealthy person, it would be easy to read Luke 12:15–21 and think it has little or nothing to say to you. But when we realize that the fallen condition is a disease that manifests a variety of symptoms depending on the person, we are reminded to ask diagnostic questions that reveal its presence in us.

Identifying the Fallen Condition

So now that we have explained what the fallen condition is, how do we go about identifying it? In some passages it is right on the surface. But in other passages it may not be as obvious. So here are some questions that can help you look for fallen conditions in a passage.

First, *what sinful tendencies, habits, thoughts, patterns of behavior, feelings, desires, or beliefs are explicitly stated in the text or reasonably implied by the text?* Let's look at Psalm 75:1:

> We give thanks to you, O God;
>> we give thanks, for your name is near.
> We recount your wondrous deeds.

This verse does not explicitly state a fallen condition. In fact, it expresses quite the opposite! But if we pause to reflect whether we always give thanks, we should realize quickly that we do not. So a fallen condition that emerges from this verse is that we fail to give thanks to God when we forget he is near. Another fallen condition might be that ingratitude grows when we fail to remember and talk about what God has done for us.

A second question that can be helpful in identifying the fallen condition is *What evidence of the effects of the fall is explicitly stated in the text or reasonably implied by it and needs the redemptive work of God?* This question helps us see consequences of the fall that are not necessarily the direct result of specific sin. Instead, they are simply the result of living in a fallen world. Take, for example, John 9:1–3:

> As he [Jesus] passed by, he saw a man blind from birth. And his disciples asked him, "Rabbi, who sinned, this man or his

> parents, that he was born blind?" Jesus answered, "It was
> not that this man sinned, or his parents, but that the works
> of God might be displayed in him."

Jesus makes it clear that being born blind was not the result of this man's sin or that of his parents. But people being born with various disabilities and illnesses is a reality in this fallen world. So the fallen condition here is simply that we live in a world where people suffer.

Let's look at another example. Sometime after the end of their first missionary journey together, Paul and Barnabas decided to return to the cities where they had planted churches.

> Now Barnabas wanted to take with them John called Mark.
> But Paul thought best not to take with them one who had
> withdrawn from them in Pamphylia and had not gone with
> them to the work. And there arose a sharp disagreement, so
> that they separated from each other. Barnabas took Mark
> with him and sailed away to Cyprus, but Paul chose Silas
> and departed, having been commended by the brothers to
> the grace of the Lord. (Acts 15:37–40)

These two godly men simply could not agree. And the passage does not settle the issue of who was right and who was wrong in this "sharp disagreement." But one consequence of living in a fallen world is that conflict is inevitable, even between believers. The fallen condition, then, is that conflict is to be expected in a world still under the effects of the curse.

Finally, we should ask *what God-given human longings, though warped by sin, are explicitly stated in the text or reasonably implied by the text and need the redemptive work of God?* When God created us, he made us with certain longings and desires. Sin, however, warps and twists them. We see a clear example of this in Genesis 16:1–2:

Now Sarai, Abram's wife, had borne him no children. She had a female Egyptian servant whose name was Hagar. And Sarai said to Abram, "Behold now, the LORD has prevented me from bearing children. Go in to my servant; it may be that I shall obtain children by her." And Abram listened to the voice of Sarai.

Sarai's desire for a child was not sinful. In fact it was part of the way God made her. Add to that God's promise to make Abram a great nation, and no wonder Sarai was desperate to have children. But sin twisted that desire to the point where instead of trusting God to fulfill his promise, she tried to take things into her own hands. The result was disastrous, as the rest of Genesis goes on to make clear. Sin took a God-given desire and warped it into a fallen condition.

An Example: 1 Thessalonians 4:13–18

Now that we have explained the fallen condition and how to identify it, let's work through an example together. In 1 Thessalonians 4:13–18, Paul writes:

> But we do not want you to be uninformed, brothers, about those who are asleep, that you may not grieve as others do who have no hope. For since we believe that Jesus died and rose again, even so, through Jesus, God will bring with him those who have fallen asleep. For this we declare to you by a word from the Lord, that we who are alive, who are left until the coming of the Lord, will not precede those who have fallen asleep. For the Lord himself will descend from heaven with a cry of command, with the voice of an archangel, and with the sound of the trumpet of God. And the dead in Christ will rise first. Then we who are alive, who are left, will be caught up together with them in the clouds to meet the Lord in the air, and so we will always

be with the Lord. Therefore encourage one another with these words.

As is true of many passages, this one has a number of different fallen conditions. Here are just four of them:

1. When we do not understand what happens to fellow believers after they die, we can grieve as those who have no hope.
2. Our grief when we respond to death shows that deep down we recognize that things are not the way they are supposed to be.
3. We can become discouraged when we think about the seeming delay in Christ's return.
4. We live our lives with little or no thought of the imminence of Christ's return, especially when our lives are comfortable.

Notice that I have tried to be specific rather than general. The more specific you can be, the more pointedly you can address the fallen condition with the gospel.

• • •

Identifying the fallen condition is crucial for applying the Bible to our lives. But it is only half of the process. Once we have determined the fallen condition, we need to figure out what God has done through the gospel to address our fallen condition. That is what we will tackle in the next chapter.

8

The Gospel Solution

Usually when you go to the doctor, it is because something is wrong with you. So a good doctor asks you a series of questions about your symptoms. From those symptoms the doctor tries to diagnose your condition.

Imagine, though, that at the end of your examination, the doctor only tells you what is wrong with you. She gives you a detailed explanation of your condition, how it is affecting your body, and what ongoing effects you can expect. She even gives you a lovely brochure that summarizes everything she has told you. But she never tells you what treatment options are available.

If a doctor only tells you what is wrong with you and never mentions how to treat it, she has only done half of her job. The role of the doctor is not only to diagnose problems but also to identify remedies.

The same is true of us when it comes to applying the Bible. Figuring out the fallen condition when reading a passage is crucial. But the Bible does more than simply show us our sin.

Scripture also shows us how God addresses our sin through the gospel. We will call this the gospel solution.

In the previous chapter, on our fallen condition, we looked at Hebrews 4:12–13. From that passage we saw that Scripture exposes our fallen condition. That passage continues:

> Since then we have a great high priest who has passed through the heavens, Jesus, the Son of God, let us hold fast our confession. For we do not have a high priest who is unable to sympathize with our weaknesses, but one who in every respect has been tempted as we are, yet without sin. Let us then with confidence draw near to the throne of grace, that we may receive mercy and find grace to help in time of need. (Heb. 4:14–16)

Because we are sinful and fallen people, God has given us a High Priest. As our High Priest, Jesus can sympathize with our weakness because he too was tempted. But unlike us, he never sinned. Because of his perfect obedience and sacrificial death on the cross, we can receive mercy and grace in our time of need. God has provided a solution to our sin through the gospel.

Understanding the Gospel Solution

So what exactly is the gospel solution? While we could explain it many different ways, here is what I mean by "gospel solution": The aspects of the gospel that are revealed in the text that provide the solution to the fallen condition. Let's unpack this definition a little further.

The gospel refers to what God has done for us in and through Jesus Christ. There are many different aspects of what Jesus has done for us. He has justified us (declared us not guilty of our sins). He has adopted us (made us part of his family). He has sanctified us (set us apart for his special purposes in the world). He has given us the Holy Spirit to live inside us. These are just a few of the different aspects of what God has done for us in the gospel through his Son, Jesus.

Just as every passage has a fallen condition, it also has a gospel solution. Sometimes that gospel solution is right within the passage itself. Take, for example, Ephesians 4:32: "Be kind to one another, tenderhearted, forgiving one another, as God in Christ forgave you." An obvious fallen condition is that we are tempted not to forgive others when they sin against us. But immediately after calling believers to forgive each other, Paul reminds us that God has already forgiven *us* in Christ. God overcomes our natural, sinful tendency to not forgive by reminding us that he has forgiven our sin through the gospel. Because we are forgiven, we are free to forgive others.

Sometimes, however, the gospel solution is not directly stated in the passage. Instead, it may be found in the larger context. In Psalm 109:1–3, David writes:

> Be not silent, O God of my praise!
> For wicked and deceitful mouths are opened against me,
>   speaking against me with lying tongues.
> They encircle me with words of hate,
>   and attack me without cause.

David goes on to call for God to bring judgment on his enemies (Ps. 109:4–20). Part of living in a fallen world as God's people is suffering persecution. But it is not until later in the psalm that we see how God addresses this particular aspect of our fallen condition:

> But you, O GOD my Lord,
>   deal on my behalf for your name's sake;
>   because your steadfast love is good, deliver me!
>   (Ps. 109:21)

Help me, O Lord my God!
> Save me according to your steadfast love!
Let them know that this is your hand;
> you, O Lord, have done it! (Ps. 109:26–27)

The answer to our suffering and persecution is that God is committed to defending the honor of his name and to delivering his people because of his steadfast love. We can trust him to care for us.

In other cases, you may have to supply the gospel solution from somewhere else in the Bible. Genesis 4:1–7 tells the story of Adam and Eve's first two sons, Cain and Abel. Let's pick up the story in verse 3:

> In the course of time Cain brought to the Lord an offering of the fruit of the ground, and Abel also brought of the firstborn of his flock and of their fat portions. And the Lord had regard for Abel and his offering, but for Cain and his offering he had no regard. So Cain was very angry, and his face fell. The Lord said to Cain, "Why are you angry, and why has your face fallen? If you do well, will you not be accepted? And if you do not do well, sin is crouching at the door. Its desire is [for] you, but you must rule over it." (Gen. 4:3–7)

The fallen condition is pretty straightforward. Sin is a hungry, predatory animal ready to devour us. But this passage nowhere explains how God solves this problem. Other parts of Scripture do, however, such as Romans 6:5–11:

> For if we have been united with him in a death like his, we shall certainly be united with him in a resurrection like his. We know that our old self was crucified with him in order that the body of sin might be brought to nothing, so that we would no longer be enslaved to sin. For one who has

died has been set free from sin. Now if we have died with Christ, we believe that we will also live with him. We know that Christ, being raised from the dead, will never die again; death no longer has dominion over him. For the death he died he died to sin, once for all, but the life he lives he lives to God. So you also must consider yourselves dead to sin and alive to God in Christ Jesus.

By faith we are united with Christ. We have died with him and therefore been set free from our slavery to sin. Sin no longer has power over us.

An Example: 1 Thessalonians 4:13–18

Let's go back now to our example passage from the previous chapter. In 1 Thessalonians 4:13–18, Paul writes:

But we do not want you to be uninformed, brothers, about those who are asleep, that you may not grieve as others do who have no hope. For since we believe that Jesus died and rose again, even so, through Jesus, God will bring with him those who have fallen asleep. For this we declare to you by a word from the Lord, that we who are alive, who are left until the coming of the Lord, will not precede those who have fallen asleep. For the Lord himself will descend from heaven with a cry of command, with the voice of an archangel, and with the sound of the trumpet of God. And the dead in Christ will rise first. Then we who are alive, who are left, will be caught up together with them in the clouds to meet the Lord in the air, and so we will always be with the Lord. Therefore encourage one another with these words.

In the last chapter we observed four different fallen conditions (FC). Now let's look at a suggested gospel solution (GS) for each of them:

FC1: When we do not understand what happens to fellow believers after they die, we can grieve as those who have no hope.

GS1: The gospel teaches us that God will gather all of his people to himself when Christ returns. Because Jesus has conquered death through his resurrection, we who are joined with him by faith have the hope of sharing in his resurrection. Therefore, even in our grief we have an unshakable hope that death does not have the final word.

FC2: Our grief when we respond to death shows that deep down we recognize that things are not the way they are supposed to be.

GS2: Through his death and resurrection, Jesus has begun to make all things new, and one day he will usher in a new heaven and new earth, where there will no longer be any curse or death.

FC3: We can become discouraged when we think about the seeming delay in Christ's return.

GS3: Because God was faithful to his promises in sending his Son to earth in the fullness of time to pay for our sin, we can be confident that God will once again send his Son to consummate his purposes for his people.

FC4: We live our lives with little or no thought of the imminence of Christ's return, especially when our lives are comfortable.

GS4: When we behold the beauty of Christ, our longing for his return will grow. As our love for Christ grows, the comforts of this world become less attractive to us. This love for Christ and his return begins to shape how we live.

These are just some of the fallen conditions and gospel solutions that one could draw from 1 Thessalonians 4:13–18. But they should be enough to give you an idea of how to find the gospel solution in a passage.

• • •

God gave us the Bible to transform us. In order for that to happen, we need to identify both the fallen condition and the gospel solution. As we grow in our understanding of the gospel, we will grow in our ability to identify how it addresses the various fallen conditions we experience. If you feel like your understanding of the gospel needs to grow, there is no substitute for reading and reflecting on Scripture itself. You might even consider keeping a journal or notebook to record what you learn about God and the gospel as you read through the Bible. Another tool you might find helpful is *A Gospel Primer for Christians: Learning to See the Glories of God's Love*, by Milton Vincent.[1] Vincent does a wonderful job of not only summarizing different aspects of the gospel, but also explaining how those different aspects have practical, everyday life implications for the way we think, feel, speak, and act.

With the fallen condition and gospel solution in place, in the next chapter we can think more specifically about how to apply the Bible to our everyday lives.

---

1. Bemidji, MN: Focus, 2008.

9

Applying the Bible
to Our Whole Lives

So far, when it comes to reading our own lives correctly, we have seen that the gospel pattern of life is one of ongoing repentance and faith. We have also learned how to expose the fallen condition and apply the gospel solution. With this foundation in place, we are now ready to think through applying the Bible to our lives.

A common problem we face when we think about applying the Bible is that our view of application is too narrow. We tend to think largely or even exclusively about what we should *do* in response to what God says in his Word. That is indeed an important aspect of application. But the Christian life is about more than what we do. Since the goal of reading and applying the Bible is life transformation, we need to make sure that we apply the Bible to our whole lives, not just actions.

How then do we do this? Once again, we will use four simple questions to help us think through the four different aspects of application.

What Does God Want Me to Think?

The first question we should ask ourselves when applying the Bible is *What does God what me to think or understand?* Before we were born again, Satan blinded our minds to prevent us from seeing the beauty of Christ, but that changed when God made us spiritually alive (2 Cor. 4:4–6). As believers, we have been given "the mind of Christ" (1 Cor. 2:16), yet we are still tempted to think the way we did before we knew Christ (Eph. 4:17–19). That is why in Romans 12:2 Paul writes, "Do not be conformed to this world, but be transformed by the renewal of your mind, that by testing you may discern what is the will of God, what is good and acceptable and perfect."

To be conformed to this world means to think, believe, desire, and act like people who do not know Christ. The world we live in constantly tries to squeeze us into its mold, inviting us to embrace its values and ideals. The antidote to this constant pressure is to be transformed. The starting point for that transformation is the renewal of our minds. God does that renewing by the Holy Spirit, who lives inside us (Titus 3:5–6).

The fact that the Holy Spirit is the one who empowers this mind renewal doesn't mean we are passive. We face a spiritual battle that requires intentional effort on our part. Paul describes it this way: "For the weapons of our warfare are not of the flesh but have divine power to destroy strongholds. We destroy arguments and every lofty opinion raised against the knowledge of God, and take every thought captive to obey Christ" (2 Cor. 10:4–5). The battle for our minds is a spiritual one. It is empowered by the Holy Spirit. Yet we are responsible to fight against every pattern of thinking that opposes or contradicts what God has said in his Word. We must take every thought captive, evaluating it against what the Bible says is true.

So when we go to apply a passage of Scripture, we want to be sure to ask what we need to understand about God, people, how to relate to God, and how to relate to others. In one sense, this is simply summarizing and reflecting on what we gained from asking the four foundational questions (see chap. 5). But asking what God wants us to think or understand also reveals incorrect ways of thinking that need to be brought in line with what the Bible says.

What Does God Want Me to Believe?

The second application question we should ask is *What does God want me to believe?* At first this question might seem like another way of asking the first question, but there is an important yet subtle difference. We can understand a truth at an intellectual level without believing it to such a degree that it shapes how we live.

A classic illustration of this is the famous French tightrope walker Charles Blondin.[1] Beginning in 1858 he performed a series of tightrope walks across Niagara Falls. Over time he became increasingly more daring. In 1859 he carried his manager, Harry Colcord, across on his back. One year later, with the Prince of Wales in the crowd, Blondin carried his assistant, Romain Mouton, across the falls on his back. When Blondin invited the Prince of Wales to ride on his back for the return trip across the tightrope, the prince declined. He understood that Blondin could safely carry him across, but did not believe it enough to jump on Blondin's back.

In Luke 8:5–8, Jesus tells a parable that helps illustrate this distinction between thinking/understanding and believing:

---

1. "Charles Blondin Biography," *Encyclopedia of World Biography*, accessed http://www.notablebiographies.com/supp/Supplement-A-Bu-and-Obituaries/Blondin-Charles.html.

"A sower went out to sow his seed. And as he sowed, some fell along the path and was trampled underfoot, and the birds of the air devoured it. And some fell on the rock, and as it grew up, it withered away, because it had no moisture. And some fell among thorns, and the thorns grew up with it and choked it. And some fell into good soil and grew and yielded a hundredfold." As he said these things, he called out, "He who has ears to hear, let him hear."

Each of the seeds stands for a different kind of response to God's Word, as Jesus goes on to explain (Luke 8:11–15):

Now the parable is this: The seed is the word of God. The ones along the path are those who have heard; then the devil comes and takes away the word from their hearts, so that they may not believe and be saved. And the ones on the rock are those who, when they hear the word, receive it with joy. But these have no root; they believe for a while, and in time of testing fall away. And as for what fell among the thorns, they are those who hear, but as they go on their way they are choked by the cares and riches and pleasures of life, and their fruit does not mature. As for that in the good soil, they are those who, hearing the word, hold it fast in an honest and good heart, and bear fruit with patience.

The seed that fell on rock represents those who hear the Word, understand it, and even receive it with joy. But they only "believe for a while" before falling away when tested. Their problem is not that they fail to understand God's Word. It is that they do not continue to believe it by basing their lives on it. By contrast, the seed that falls on good soil represents those who hear the Word, understand it, and "hold it fast in an honest and good heart." In other words, they believe it by basing how they live on it.

This distinction between thinking/understanding and believing appears often in the New Testament letters. Much of what is in these letters is not brand-new information but rather reminders of what the readers already knew. In Ephesians 2:11–22, Paul commands his readers to remember a whole series of truths he taught them before. His point is to call the Ephesians to believe the truth they have already understood in such a way that it shapes how they live.

A major reason that God gave us his Word is to produce faith in us. According to Romans 10:17, "faith comes from hearing, and hearing through the word of Christ." Asking what God wants us to believe gives us an opportunity to identify the false beliefs that motivate our sinful actions. That puts us in position to confess those false beliefs and move forward in believing what God says is true.

What Does God Want Me to Desire?

The third application question to ask is *What does God want me to desire?* This question gets at what the eighteenth-century preacher Jonathan Edwards called the affections. He saw the affections as the spring (that is, the source and power) of our actions. So our desires are central to our affections. The Bible often tells us where our desires should or should not be directed.

> As a deer pants for flowing streams,
>   so pants my soul for you, O God.
> My soul thirsts for God,
>   for the living God.
> When shall I come and appear before God? (Ps. 42:1–2)

> Be not envious of evil men,
>   nor desire to be with them,

for their hearts devise violence,
>   and their lips talk of trouble. (Prov. 24:1–2)

The affections also include our inclinations. Each of us has certain natural tendencies, but we are also responsible before God for cultivating the right kind of inclinations. Our natural inclinations are toward sin and idolatry. But as part of the transforming work of his Spirit, God uses the Bible to reorient our inclinations and tendencies toward him and his ways. That is why David prays:

Teach me your way, O Lord,
>   that I may walk in your truth;
>   unite my heart to fear your name.
I give thanks to you, O Lord my God,
>   with my whole heart,
>   and I will glorify your name forever. (Ps. 86:11–12)

When we think about what God wants us to desire, we should also consider our emotions. Well-meaning people may have told you that no one has the right to tell you how to feel. But God certainly has no problem telling us how we should feel. When reading the Bible, we should have an emotional response to what God is saying. In some passages, that response is explicitly stated:

Be angry, and do not sin;
>   ponder in your own hearts on your beds, and be silent.
>   (Ps. 4:4)

I will give thanks to the Lord with my whole heart;
>   I will recount all of your wonderful deeds.
I will be glad and exult in you;
>   I will sing praise to your name, O Most High.
>   (Ps. 9:1–2)

Why are you cast down, O my soul,
   and why are you in turmoil within me?
Hope in God; for I shall again praise him,
   my salvation and my God. (Ps. 42:5)

In other passages, however, an emotional response may be implied rather than stated directly: "And whoever gives one of these little ones even a cup of cold water because he is a disciple, truly, I say to you, he will by no means lose his reward" (Matt. 10:42). When we read this, we should feel encouraged that God sees and rewards even our smallest acts of kindness toward others. But we also might feel convicted that our motivation to serve others comes from a desire to earn their approval. Asking how God wants us to feel helps us engage the Bible at the heart level. Even if we are not currently experiencing a similar situation in our own lives, the text should still move us at an emotional level. We may not be currently grieving over a difficult situation in our lives, but we can likely enter into the grief of someone we know. Doing so can stir compassion in our hearts for others and may even lead us to pray for or encourage someone who is grieving.

Asking what God wants us to desire can reveal sinful desires, inclinations, and feelings that the Holy Spirit needs to change. If we do not desire what God says we should desire, then we should confess this and pursue repentance. As God shows us who or what we should desire, we can pray for his Spirit to change us so that our desires, inclinations, and feelings line up with what Scripture says.

What Does God Want Me to Do?

Our fourth and final application question is *What does God want me to do?* Some passages in the Bible give us direct commands on what we should do as followers of Christ. Take, for example, this series of rapid-fire instructions:

> Let love be genuine. Abhor what is evil; hold fast to what is good. Love one another with brotherly affection. Outdo one another in showing honor. Do not be slothful in zeal, be fervent in spirit, serve the Lord. Rejoice in hope, be patient in tribulation, be constant in prayer. Contribute to the needs of the saints and seek to show hospitality.
>
> Bless those who persecute you; bless and do not curse them. Rejoice with those who rejoice, weep with those who weep. Live in harmony with one another. Do not be haughty, but associate with the lowly. Never be wise in your own sight. Repay no one evil for evil, but give thought to do what is honorable in the sight of all. (Rom. 12:9–17)

Coming up with specific actions that would apply this passage to our lives is not hard. In fact, we might feel overwhelmed with all God wants us to do from this passage!

But a number of passages are far less straightforward. Here is where it is especially important to remember that Scripture was written for us, not to us. So we have to be careful about drawing a straight line from actions commanded in the text. This is especially true when we read the Old Testament. Consider Leviticus 19:9–10:

> When you reap the harvest of your land, you shall not reap your field right up to its edge, neither shall you gather the gleanings after your harvest. And you shall not strip your vineyard bare, neither shall you gather the fallen grapes of your vineyard. You shall leave them for the poor and for the sojourner: I am the LORD your God.

When the Israelites went to harvest their crops, God commanded them to leave some behind so the poor and sojourners could gather the leftovers. But as we read this today, we need to keep in mind that we are not Israelites and, more importantly, we are not under the Mosaic covenant. So it would be misguided for us to conclude that God wants us to leave behind some of the vegetables in our garden. But we might conclude that God wants us to give toward a local ministry that helps meet the needs of the poor.

Asking what God wants us to do helps us recognize actions we should be taking but are not. It also exposes sinful actions we should stop doing. Some actions that God brings to mind are occasional, but others may be far more habitual. Pursuing repentance for repeated and habitual sin often requires help and encouragement from other believers. When we identify areas of sin, we should always be sure to root the desired new actions in our transformed thoughts, beliefs, and desires.

• • •

The goal of understanding the Bible and applying it to our lives is life transformation. We want God's Spirit to use God's Word to make us more like God's Son. These four aspects of application—thinking, believing, desiring, and doing—put us in position to see God produce deep and lasting change in our lives.

Ready to try it out? At the end of chapter 5 I suggested reading through Matthew 8 and working through the four foundational questions. Why not go back to Matthew 8 with these four application questions and see what God wants you to think, believe, desire, and do? Why not take notes as you go? Pray for God to guide you as you try to apply the passage to your life.

10

The Power to Obey

By now, I hope you are excited and eager to read the Bible and apply it to your life. Armed with the four foundational questions (from chap. 5), the four aspects of application (from chap. 9), and an understanding of the fallen condition and gospel solution (chaps. 7 and 8), you're ready to dive into God's Word. Along with David you believe that it is

> more to be desired . . . than gold,
> > even much fine gold;
> sweeter also than honey
> > and drippings of the honeycomb. (Ps. 19:10)

So it may seem strange to say that just when you are most excited to apply the Bible to your life, you are in danger of making a common mistake in Christian living. With our focus on what tools we can use to grow in our relationship with God and others, we can begin to think that becoming more like Christ is something we can produce by our own efforts.

Paul addresses a similar issue in Galatians. He asks his

readers a rhetorical question to remind them of a crucial spiritual truth: "Having begun by the Spirit, are you now being perfected by the flesh?" (Gal. 3:3).

The Galatians were being told that, while believing the gospel is how the Christian life begins, their growth in the Christian life depended on their own efforts to obey the Mosaic law. But just as we cannot make ourselves right with God based on our own efforts, we cannot grow in godliness through our own efforts.

Yet we must also avoid the opposite mistake of thinking that we are completely passive when it comes to our spiritual growth. All throughout the Bible (including the New Testament) there are countless commands that God expects us to obey. Explaining the nature of his ministry, Paul says that he has "received grace and apostleship to bring about the obedience of faith for the sake of his name among all the nations" (Rom. 1:5). A central goal of Paul's ministry is to lead people to a growing obedience to God that flows from their faith in Christ.

When Jesus commissions his followers to take the gospel to the ends of the earth, he also emphasizes the goal of obedience:

> And Jesus came and said to them, "All authority in heaven and on earth has been given to me. Go therefore and make disciples of all nations, baptizing them in the name of the Father and of the Son and of the Holy Spirit, teaching them to observe all that I have commanded you. And behold, I am with you always, to the end of the age." (Matt. 28:18–20)

Obedience to all that Jesus commands requires intentional effort and action, not passively waiting for God to zap us into godliness.

So how should we think through the relationship between God's role in our spiritual growth and ours? An excellent starting point is Philippians 2:12–13.

A Key Passage: Philippians 2:12–13

Paul had a very close relationship with the church at Philippi. In the midst of reminding the Philippians of his love for them and the beauty of Jesus Christ, Paul writes:

> Therefore, my beloved, as you have always obeyed, so now, not only as in my presence but much more in my absence, work out your own salvation with fear and trembling, for it is God who works in you, both to will and to work for his good pleasure. (Phil. 2:12–13)

Paul tells believers to work out our own salvation. But he also stresses that God is the one at work in us for his good pleasure. So even though Paul begins with our responsibility ("work out your own salvation with fear and trembling"), he grounds it in what God has done and is doing ("for it is God who works in you"). Let's look at each of these, starting with God's work.

God's Work

Paul lists two specific things God does. First, he produces *the desire to obey him.* Looking ahead to the new covenant, God promised to give his redeemed people a new heart and write his law on our renewed hearts:

> And I will give you a new heart, and a new spirit I will put within you. And I will remove the heart of stone from your flesh and give you a heart of flesh. (Ezek. 36:26)

> For this is the covenant that I will make with the house of Israel after those days, declares the LORD: I will put my law

within them, and I will write it on their hearts. And I will be their God, and they shall be my people. (Jer. 31:33)

Because of what Jesus has done for us, we experience these blessings of the new covenant. On top of that, Christ also transforms us from being slaves to sin into slaves of God: "But now that you have been set free from sin and have become slaves of God, the fruit you get leads to sanctification and its end, eternal life" (Rom. 6:22). Through the work of the gospel, God gives his people the desire to obey him.

Second, God gives us *the power to obey him*. Before we know Christ, we are unable to obey God. Note what Romans 8:7–8 says: "For the mind that is set on the flesh is hostile to God, for it does not submit to God's law; indeed, it cannot. Those who are in the flesh cannot please God." But speaking of the new covenant, God promised to enable his redeemed people to obey them. Let's go back to Ezekiel 36 and look at verse 27 this time: "And I will put my Spirit within you, and cause you to walk in my statutes and be careful to obey my rules."

Romans 8:11 sheds further light on what the Holy Spirit does in our lives: "If the Spirit of him who raised Jesus from the dead dwells in you, he who raised Christ Jesus from the dead will also give life to your mortal bodies through his Spirit who dwells in you." The life that God gives us refers not only to the future resurrection of our bodies but also to the new spiritual life we experience in the present. One of the most important things the Holy Spirit does in the life of the believer is empower us to walk in obedience. In Romans 8:13, Paul writes, "For if you live according to the flesh you will die, but if by the Spirit you put to death the deeds of the body, you will live." As believers we have the Spirit of God giving us the ability to obey God.

All three persons of the Trinity are involved in the work of life transformation. The Father calls his children to be holy as he is holy (1 Pet. 1:14–17) and predestines us "to be conformed to the image of his Son" (Rom. 8:29). Thus the Son is the ultimate pattern of God's work in our lives, and it is his work on the cross that makes conformity to him even possible. Through our union with him we share in his death and resurrection, and are therefore able to walk in newness of life (Rom 6:1–11). The Spirit is the one who applies the benefits of Christ's work to us, and this includes the application of Scripture to our Christian walk. He produces fruit in our lives that reflects the character of Christ himself (Gal. 5:22–24).

Our Work

Growth in godliness does not come by waiting for God to zap us. A helpful starting point for thinking about our role is Paul's statement in Romans 10:17: "So faith comes from hearing, and hearing through the word of Christ." We work out our own salvation by believing the good news about Jesus Christ and his work on our behalf.

We also pray for God to reveal sin in our lives and change our thoughts, beliefs, desires, and actions, perhaps along the lines of Psalm 19:12–14:

Who can discern his errors?
Declare me innocent from hidden faults.
Keep back your servant also from presumptuous sins;
let them not have dominion over me!
Then I shall be blameless,
and innocent of great transgression.

Let the words of my mouth and the meditation of
my heart
be acceptable in your sight,
O Lord, my rock and my redeemer.

Prayer aligns us with God's will as we confess our sins and beg for him to transform us into the image of Jesus Christ.

God has also given us fellow believers to encourage and stimulate us to turn from our sins, trust in God's promises, and pursue good works. Hebrews 10:23–25 captures this reality well:

> Let us hold fast the confession of our hope without wavering, for he who promised is faithful. And let us consider how to stir up one another to love and good works, not neglecting to meet together, as is the habit of some, but encouraging one another, and all the more as you see the Day drawing near.

Other believers can often point out our blind spots, as well as confront and encourage us when necessary. As we live in fellowship with other believers, we are able to grow together in godliness.

• • •

Whether you are excited to take the tools you have learned or a little nervous about using them, you can move forward with the confidence that God has given you both the desire and the power to obey him. As you learn to practice the pattern of repentance and faith over time, you will begin to see spiritual growth in your life. God will use your faithful and consistent involvement in the local church to encourage, comfort, and challenge you in your relationship with him.

It certainly will not be easy. You have sinful desires and inclinations to wage war against. You live in a world that is in rebellion against God and his ways. Your enemy Satan seeks your destruction. But let these passages of Scripture be your comfort:

I have said these things to you, that in me you may have peace. In the world you will have tribulation. But take heart; I have overcome the world. (John 16:33)

Little children, you are from God and have overcome them, for he who is in you is greater than he who is in the world. (1 John 4:4)

For everyone who has been born of God overcomes the world. And this is the victory that has overcome the world— our faith. Who is it that overcomes the world except the one who believes that Jesus is the Son of God? (1 John 5:4–5)

Conclusion

The Bible is unlike any other book. Throughout the centuries God's people have found comfort, joy, instruction, correction, and food for their souls. Listen to how King David describes it in Psalm 19:7–11:

> The law of the Lord is perfect,
>   reviving the soul;
> the testimony of the Lord is sure,
>   making wise the simple;
> the precepts of the Lord are right,
>   rejoicing the heart;
> the commandment of the Lord is pure,
>   enlightening the eyes;
> the fear of the Lord is clean,
>   enduring forever;
> the rules of the Lord are true,
>   and righteous altogether.
> More to be desired are they than gold,
>   even much fine gold;
> sweeter also than honey
>   and drippings of the honeycomb.
> Moreover, by them is your servant warned;
>   in keeping them there is great reward.

Reviving the soul. Making wise the simple. Rejoicing the heart. Enlightening the eyes. More to be desired than fine gold. When you hold your Bible in your hands, you are holding a treasure far greater than anything this world offers. The Bible is a treasure because it shows us who God is, who we are, and how we should live. It lays out the story that we live in, the true story of the world. It shows us the beauty of Jesus Christ, who is the fullest revelation of God's glory.

You now have a set of tools to help you understand the Bible and apply it to your everyday life. Whether you are a new believer, a Christian who wants to grow in your relationship with God through his Word, or someone entrusted with helping others understand and apply the Bible, God wants to deepen your relationship with him through the Bible.

After telling a series of parables, Jesus said this to his disciples: "Therefore every scribe who has been trained for the kingdom of heaven is like a master of a house, who brings out of his treasure what is new and what is old" (Matt. 13:52). My prayer for you is that as you learn to ask the right questions, you too will be like the master of a house who is able to bring out treasures new and old from God's Word.

ADDITIONAL RESOURCES

Tips for Understanding and Applying Different Kinds of Passages

The Bible contains various kinds of literature (narratives, poetry, parables, and so forth), sometimes referred to as genres. Using the approach laid out in this book works no matter what kind of passage you are reading. But it helps to keep some specific things in mind when reading these different genres. So while this list is not exhaustive, these tips can help you understand and apply the Bible faithfully. If you want more help with these different genres, consider checking out Robert L. Plummer, *40 Questions about Interpreting the Bible*.[1]

Narrative. Much of the Bible is in narrative form, telling stories about key people and events. When reading a narrative, pay attention to the larger context (the stories before and

---

1. Grand Rapids, MI: Kregel, 2010.

after it) and look for key themes and repetition in the narrative. Look at what the characters do and how they are described. If the author includes an editorial comment of sorts, it often indicates something important.

When you move to application, be careful not to assume we should just imitate the actions of the characters. Do not assume that everything a character does in the story is approved by God. Sometimes narratives record the sinful actions of individuals without specifically identifying those actions as sinful. Try to distinguish what is specific to that particular event/story and what principles transcend it.

Law. Significant sections of the Old Testament contain laws and regulations that Israel was commanded to obey. But since as Christians we are under the new covenant, these laws and regulations do not apply to us directly. So the first question to ask when you read the laws and regulations in the Old Testament is whether or not the New Testament comments on or repeats them in some fashion. If so, let the New Testament passage determine what a law means and how it applies.

If a particular Old Testament law is not mentioned in the New Testament, try to determine the basic principle behind it. Even the Old Testament laws that do not apply to us directly can teach us about who God is, who we are, and how we should live.

Poetry. The Old Testament (as well as a few places in the New Testament) has large sections of poetry. The Psalms are the most obvious example, but the prophetic books are also dominated by poetry. A key feature of poetry is parallelism, where an idea stated in the first line is then further developed in the second line. You should also expect figures of speech such as metaphors and similes. Poetry is intended to provoke an emotional response, so do not be surprised if your application is heavy on the desire aspect.

Proverbs and Wisdom Literature. Wisdom Literature (Job, Proverbs, Ecclesiastes, Song of Solomon) describes in various ways how the world typically works. When reading proverbs, be sure to remember that they are general statements and not necessarily ironclad promises. Avoid reading individual statements in the Wisdom Books without looking at the larger context of each book. Always compare what you read in the Wisdom Books with what the rest of the Bible says to make sure you are not misunderstanding it.

Parables. Although there are a few parables in the Old Testament, most are located in the Gospels. Some parables are short statements similar to proverbs, while others are short stories. Jesus told parables to explain spiritual realities about the kingdom of God. Pay attention to the characters and the imagery in a parable. Be sure to look at the larger context when reading the parable. Sometimes there is an explanation of what the parable means. Parables are often grouped together around a key theme or themes. Be careful not press every single detail in a parable for some deep spiritual meaning.

Prophecy and apocalyptic literature. Prophecy (e.g., Isaiah, Jeremiah, Ezekiel) and apocalyptic literature (e.g., Revelation, sections of Daniel) are some of the hardest parts of Scripture to understand and apply. It can be challenging to know whether prophecy refers to an event or a person in the immediate future, the distant future, or even at the end of human history. Sometimes the answer is all of the above!

Often prophecy and apocalyptic literature stress God's sovereign judgment on sin but also his staggering mercy for those who repent and believe. As best you can, pay attention to what God promises and how those promises have been fulfilled (in part or in whole) later in Scripture, especially in Jesus Christ and his people.

Letters/Epistles. Over half of the New Testament books are letters or epistles. In some respects letters are among the easiest books of the Bible to understand and apply. When reading a New Testament letter, look for key themes and repeated words, ideas, or concepts. Since each letter was written to a specific person, church, or group of churches, pay attention to the situation and challenges the recipient(s) faced. Try to follow the larger argument of the letter so you can correctly understand individual verses and paragraphs. Be sure to pay attention to both what the author says God has done for us in Christ and what he commands us to do as his obedient children.

A Word to Pastors, Sunday School Teachers, and Small Group Leaders

Helping others understand the Bible and apply it to their lives is a great privilege and a great responsibility. The starting point is making sure that we understand a passage and apply it to our own lives first. When people see that we have obeyed the text ourselves, they are far more likely to apply it to their own lives.

When it comes to helping others apply the Bible, we should begin by asking the questions for the four aspects of application. But there are two additional categories to think through when seeking to apply the Bible to the lives of others.

Analyze Your Audience

When it comes to applying the Bible to others, we need to understand the people we are leading. The smaller the group, the easier it usually is to know them well enough to make targeted application. But if you teach a large Sunday school class or preach to a larger group of people, you may not know every individual in your audience. Regardless of how well you know the audience, the starting point is a good working knowledge of the fallen condition in the passage. Try to be as specific as possible about the fallen condition. Think through examples that illustrate how the fallen condition might show up in different ways in the lives of different people.

When thinking about your audience, several factors are helpful to consider. Gender is a good place to start. The way a fallen condition works itself out in the life of a woman may differ from how it shows up in the life of a man. Cultural circumstances and values within a person's ethnic background/context can often influence how a fallen condition manifests itself, as well as the gospel solution. The same is true of socioeconomic status, spiritual maturity, and a person's life stage or status (i.e., child, teen, college student, married, single, parent, retired, etc.). These categories work in combination to shape how the fallen condition plays out in a person's life. As a result they will also shape some of the specifics of application for the various people in your audience.

Reflect on Individual and Corporate Applications

As Westerners we tend to default to thinking about application in individualistic terms. Through the gospel God calls individuals to repent and believe, as well as to obey him. But when God saves us, he saves us into a body of believers—the church. Scripture often addresses how the people of God live as a group, not merely as individuals.

So when thinking about how to apply a passage to the people you lead, be sure to consider how it applies to the corporate life of your small group, class, and/or congregation. Think through what the passage has to say about the way believers should live together as the church. Are there truths that the entire group of believers needs to partner together to obey? What does the passage say about how we should interact with each other and with those outside the church?

A Brief Example

Let's consider an example. In 2 Corinthians 8–9, Paul addresses the issue of giving. In one of the key sections of these two chapters he writes:

> Each one must give as he has decided in his heart, not reluctantly or under compulsion, for God loves a cheerful giver. And God is able to make all grace abound to you, so that having all sufficiency in all things at all times, you may abound in every good work. (9:7–8)

An obvious fallen condition is that our natural tendency to look out for ourselves prevents us from cheerfully and self-sacrificially giving. Although the focus of the passage is financial giving, applying the passage goes beyond that kind of giving to include time and other resources.

For a teenage girl growing up in a middle-class family, the fallen condition might show itself in complete ignorance of the needs of those who live in her community. A young married couple with large amounts of student debt might think they cannot afford to give because it would take away money they could use to pay off that debt. A wealthy small-business owner may be giving simply to enhance his reputation in the church or the community.

What about applying this passage to the corporate life of the church? When it comes to budgeting, a church can so prioritize its own wants that it neglects giving to others. Or perhaps a church focuses its giving toward local agencies and ministries to help enhance its reputation in the community while neglecting international opportunities. God can use a passage like this to help the church evaluate not only the amount of their giving but also their motivations.

• • •

The more specific you can be, the more clearly you and the people you lead will be able to see the fallen condition at work. When you give specific examples that reveal the presence of the fallen condition, people will recognize their own thoughts, attitudes, and actions in what you are describing. The more specific you are in identifying the fallen condition, the more precision you will have in applying the gospel solution. The better you know the specific people you are leading, as well as the larger cultural influences that feed the fallen condition you have identified, the better you will be able to speak God's Word into their lives.

A friend of mine once referred to this as "reading people's mail." In other words, when you identify the fallen condition and how it shows up in a person's life, you want the person to have that moment where he or she thinks, "That's totally what I think/believe/desire/do." Once someone reaches that point, the gospel solution will seem especially sweet.

At a Glance

Asking the Right Questions

Sometimes it helps to have a simple summary of "the right questions" to ask when interpreting and applying Scripture. On the following page are the four foundational questions for understanding the Bible and the four aspects of application (from chap. 5, "Four Foundational Questions," and chap. 9, "Applying the Bible to Our Whole Lives"). You might even consider copying the summary page and placing it in your Bible to refer to while you read God's Word.

• • •

Understanding the Bible

1. What do we learn about God?
   a. Look for God's *character* (who he is, what he is like).
   b. Look for God's *conduct* (what he is doing).
   c. Look for God's *concerns* (what things, events, people, he is concerned about).

2. What do we learn about people?
   a. Look for aspects of what it means to be *created in God's image.*
   b. Look for the *fallen condition.*
   c. Look for *how God's people should live.*

3. What do we learn about relating to God?
   a. Look for things to *praise and thank God for.*
   b. Look for sin to *confess and repent.*
   c. Look for *promises and truths to believe.*

4. What do we learn about relating to others?
   a. Look for how we should *interact with and treat others.*
   b. Look for ways to *pursue reconciliation with others.*
   c. Look for specific ways to *love, serve, and care for others.*

Applying the Bible

1. What does God want me to *think/understand*?
2. What does God want me to *believe*?
3. What does God want me to *desire*?
4. What does God want me to *do*?

General Index

Abraham, covenant with, 23
actions, 108–9
Adam, covenant with, 23
Adam and Eve
    commission of, 20–21, 24, 34
    rebellion of, 21–22, 36, 66–67
adoption, 94
affection, 105–7
apocalyptic literature, 125–26
applying the Bible, 13–15, 101–9,
    127–30
asking questions, 63, 101–9,
    131–32
audience, knowledge of, 128

believing, 70, 80, 103–4
Bible
    continuity and discontinuity
      in, 51
    deepens understanding, 52
    God's tool for renewal, 39–42
    and life transformation, 99,
      101, 109
    points to Jesus Christ, 46–47,
      50
    produces faith, 105
    reading of, 45–53
    as a story, 19–20, 51, 63–64
    as treasure, 120

as variety of literature, 123
as written for us but not to us,
    55–61
Blondin, Charles, 103

Cain and Abel, 96
Chapell, Bryan, 87
Christian life
    entry point into, 81–82
    growth in, 112
    pattern for, 15–16, 78, 82–84
church, 30, 128–29
commitment, 80
community, 21
confession, 69–70
conflict, 72
consummation, 31, 59
covenants, 23–28
creation, 20–21
crisis, 21–23
curse, 22

David
    affections of, 106
    on the Bible, 119
    care for Mephibosheth, 72
    covenant with, 25–26
    on Word of God, 40–41, 111
    death, 22
deceitful desires, 70

Scripture Index

.